ING

have
s.’

A TRUE KNOWING

Drawn from Sermons & Writings
Salisbury 1977–1986

SYDNEY EVANS
Dean of Salisbury

Edited by Suzanne Eward

Foreword by the Right Revd John Austin Baker
Bishop of Salisbury

MICHAEL RUSSELL

First published in Great Britain 1990
by Michael Russell (Publishing) Ltd
The Chantry, Wilton, Salisbury, Wiltshire
Typeset by The Typesetting Bureau
Wimborne, Dorset
Printed and bound in Great Britain
by Biddles Ltd, Guildford and King's Lynn

0 85955 173 3

Foreword

The sermons which Sydney Evans preached during his years as Dean of Salisbury, and from which this anthology is taken, were to a unique degree a distillation of the message God had given him for the general people of Christ.

Though themes recur which are familiar in addresses from his earlier career in London, they are not directed here, as they were there, to the special needs of the ordained or of those in training for ordination, of the academic community or of members of the wide range of professions to which in his life he acted as a spiritual mentor. The manifold interests and enthusiasms of his mind – science, art, poetry, history – are still vividly present but not as the way in for the message, rather as the setting in which any serious person of our time must live. For that is what this anthology is about: living as a truly human person.

Some preachers, perhaps the majority, work by inducting you into a special world, the world of the Bible story and of Christian affirmations drawn from that, and then saying 'What does that mean for us today?' They take you first to another, unfamiliar place and then bring you back – or try to.

Such was not Sydney's method. Sydney starts in the world where you are, and tries to help you to see it differently, to see it in fact as it really is, not as custom or apathy or even conventional religion colour it to be.

For Sydney the mystery of human uniqueness, the definition of the human condition, is that we are beings 'who have to do with God'. What that God is, we discover when we look at the world and our relationships in the light of Jesus Christ. That for him is the heavenly vision: not just the face of Jesus, but the world seen clearly for the first time as a result of seeing Jesus. 'True knowing' is not simply knowing God in the person of Christ but knowing all things as beloved creatures of the God discovered more and more deeply day by day through Christ.

This 'true knowing' certainly includes finding true words to express true thoughts about God and his world, because no more for his dear cathedral congregation than for his students and academic colleagues of earlier years would Sydney abate the demands of the mind. All of us need to face the riddles and doubts of existence to the best of our capacity if we are to be authentic and honourable men and women.

But if one motif stands out more than any other in these pages it is that true knowing is more than analysing and defining. It is also, and quite fundamentally, *being* and *doing*. The vision changes us by revealing Love where we had never suspected it or had even determined in despair that it could not be; and that Love lays upon us a demand which we may try to evade or forget but which once acknowledged can never, short of spiritual suicide, be rooted out.

So it is that the sermons, whatever the starting-point of each, all inexorably home in on this business of living as a person in the actual world, on what kind of person in what quality of relationships we are, on the responsibilities – whether political, family, environmental, individual – which divine Love reveals by the light it throws on to and into our fellow creatures and ourselves. But the sermons are Gospel sermons, 'Good News', because they speak of a Love that does not condemn, but accepts, believes, trusts, and so draws us to better than our former best.

This core truth of the Christian message is illumined by many examples from recognisable workaday experience. Yet the deepest reason why these pages speak with authority is that they are the honest voice of the preacher's own pilgrimage. Sydney tells it as it is because he has been there, both in prayer and in action. He knew, none better, that reticence is a necessary guardian of the soul. Here are neither anecdotes of personal achievement nor a flaunting of personal failure. But the sensitive reader, whether or not he met Sydney in the days of his flesh, quickly discovers here a guide who can testify from a 'true knowing' of his own heart to the transforming reality both of divine grace and of our need of grace. Many will turn and return to what is written here because in the writer they will come to know, to love and to trust one who was 'not disobedient to the heavenly vision'.

✠ JOHN SARUM

If I were to ask what your attitude is to times past and the exploration of times past, I would expect a variety of answers. For some the past is dead and of little interest; for others the past is prologue to the present and full of fascination. For some the past tells of 'old unhappy far-off things and battles long ago'; for others the past is the prolific treasury of art and architecture, music and artefacts that immeasurably enrich our life today; for yet others a Chaucerian kaleidoscope, a colourful pageant of many-splendoured personalities. For some the study and reading of history is a safe world in which to move, a refuge from the political and emotional complexities of the present. For others tradition is the seedbed of creativity – in the arts and in literature, certainly, a fertile source of enlightenment and enrichment.

When I first came to Salisbury as Dean, the name of John of Salisbury meant no more to me than the name of the author of a quotation that made me want one day to know more about the author. Asked to lecture to the Friends on their Festival Day, I offered as subject 'John of Salisbury: Man of Letters', knowing that the prospect of execution concentrates the mind wonderfully. He died as Bishop of Chartres in 1180; his world began in the world of Old Sarum, the world out of which was to come our own Cathedral, the world with which in continuity we are still linked by our Cathedral School which has grown out of Bishop Osmund's song school and grammar school on the old hill-fort made fortress by the Normans, half castle and half church of God. The east window designed and made in Chartres by Gabriel Loire links us with the Chartres where John of Salisbury died more than 800 years ago.

The quotation which set all this going in my mind comes from one of the 325 Latin letters written by John of Salisbury. Oddly the person to whom this particular letter was addressed is not named. It expresses the importance to John of personal friendship and his high expectations of it.

Cruel Fortune grudges me the happiness for which I long and too often resists the efforts of my tender love. The treasure of my heart has long been stored in the region where you dwell, and lodged with you I have that which I count most precious in all the world, an abundance of faithful friends. If I have been deceived, the error into which my credulity, so rudely shaken, has led me, is one which I cannot regret. For our judgement of the character of our friends should always be a sacred thing, and worthy of all respect; to misjudge them too readily argues perversity of mind. I am right in speaking of the abundance of my friends, because I love many and I am sure that many in return love me. I am sure, I say, because I do not question the certainty of my hope, and know that it does not mislead me, because in the end love is never confounded. Although from time to time it is led astray by simplicity of conscience, it escapes confusion, since grace and perfect virtue come to its aid. What therefore can be sweeter than to visit such treasure again and yet again, when the soul is filled with joy and makes others share that joy? 'Where love is, there is the eye,' and 'where your treasure is, there the heart is also.' What can be more bitter than to be debarred from gazing on that which melts the heart or goes home to it beyond all else, and towards which the ray of vision is always directed? I have long been afflicted by this bitterness, the bitterest of all; for I have not been able to see any of my friends in your house.

Professor Colin Morris, in his *The Discovery of the Individual, 1050-1200*, speaks of the twelfth century as the 'century of friendship'. A century better known to us for the ecstasy and agony of Heloise and Peter Abelard was also a century in which the art and practice of friendship created a net of relationships all over western Europe linking men of common mind. Certainly John of Salisbury's capacity for friendship comes out again and again in his letters, especially those to Peter of Celle, who was to succeed him as Bishop of Chartres.

Friendship was no new discovery. In the Old Testament literature, in Proverbs and Psalms especially, are to be found memorable expressions like 'There is a friend that sticketh closer than a brother'; 'Faithful are the wounds of a friend'. And the exquisite experience of friendship is all the more enhanced by the terrible experience of being betrayed by a friend. 'Mine own familiar friend, whom I trusted: who did also eat of my bread, hath laid great wait for me.' 'And if one asks him "What are these wounds on your back?", he will say "The wounds I received in the house of my friends".' Matthew gives Jesus's response to the betraying kiss of Judas in the words 'Friend, why are you here?' And in all art surely there is no other painting that captures the intensity of betrayal by a friend as the painting of this scene by Giotto in the Arena chapel in Padua.

From the classical world Cicero's attractive dialogue on friendship, *De Amicitia*, has been read and read again. Bernard of Clairvaux urged Aelred of Rievaulx to write about friendship and there are unmistakable connections between Cicero's book and Aelred's; but Aelred's carried the significant title *Spiritual Friendship*.

And when Hildebert, Archbishop of Tours, wrote to Bernard of Clairvaux in admiration expressing his great desire to be admitted 'to the sanctity of your friendship', Bernard replied: 'Such as I am, I am yours.'

To understand the secret of this very special quality of friendship which shone like a jewel among the darker colours of the medieval world we must understand its Christ-centredness. What drew men together was their participation in the love of Christ. Aelred understood friendship as an encounter with God: 'He who dwells in friendship dwells in God and God in him.' And this is all of a piece with Bernard's analysis of the four stages of love which begins and ends in different kinds of self-love. His teaching is designed to explain how the love of God can permeate and direct all our loves. First comes loving self for self's sake; then loving God for self's sake; then loving God for God's sake; then loving self for God's sake.

Expanded, his argument is this. God manifests his goodness by condescending to our concern about ourselves; God meets our self-needs so that from the sterility of self-love for self's sake we may pass to love God for what he does for us. And this liberates us for loving others with proportion, fairness, accuracy ('iustitia' is Bernard's word). Our perspectives are broadened, 'our hearts', as St Benedict puts it, 'expand'. Gradually human love is purified; we begin to love more generously, more as we are loved, the more we 'seek the things that belong to Christ'. Thus our hearts come to love God for his own sake, for what he is, not only for what he does. But this is not the end. We have to return to deal with ourselves for God's sake. This is to love the self we are to become, the self God desires for us; and so comes the final purging of our will from self-aggrandisement and desire for control.

Within the matrix of this spiritual gestation the medieval understanding of friendship grew. But perhaps there is no more tender expression of this deep inwardness of friendship in and through Christ than in a poem written in the ninth century by Hrabanus Maurus to Grimold, Abbot of St Gall - beautifully rendered into English by Helen Waddell:

> Then live, my strength, anchor of weary ships,
> Safe shore and land at last, thou, for my wreck,
> My honour, thou, and my abiding rest,
> My city safe for a bewildered heart.
> What though the plains and mountains and the sea
> Between us are, that which no earth can hold
> Still follows thee, and love's own singing follows,
> Longing that all things may be well with thee.
> Christ who first gave thee for a friend to me,
> Christ keep thee well, where'er thou art, for me.
> Earth's self shall go and the swift wheel of heaven
> Perish and pass, before our love shall cease.
> Do but remember me, as I do thee,
> And God, who brought us on this earth together,
> Bring us together in His house of heaven.

If you were the editor of a newspaper with pen poised on 30 December 1999 preparing to write your last leading article of the twentieth century, and if you had a mind to select for your comment the persons who seemed most sharply to symbolise the century now ending, whom would you choose? Would you choose the astronaut, the entertainer, the scientist, the technologist, the tycoon, the athlete? I would choose the political prisoner – the prisoner of conscience.

Science and technology have radically changed our ways of experiencing life and our style of living. But at a deeper level human beings and human society are more or less as they have always been. That is why in the twentieth century the political prisoner is profoundly significant and symbolic because the political prisoner is profoundly significant in every century. From Socrates and Jeremiah to Paul and Polycarp, from Tyndale and Thomas More to Bonhoeffer and Solzhenitsyn, he represents humanity in search of integrity. Here is the man or the woman who challenges the essential lie, the essential untruth, the destructive falsehood that erodes true human and moral and social values. The prisoner of conscience suffers imprisonment and death rather than compromise the truth as he sees it.

In every century there have been such men and women, non-Christian as well as Christian, but in no previous century have there been so many. Perhaps this is the best thing that can be said about it in the long march of everyman. Thousands of these valiant men and women are unknown and unrecorded. They have spoken to the human conscience of their contemporaries by the silent witness of suffering and death. But an articulate few have put on paper what they have intended, why they have suffered. Such writers compel our attention by the integrity of words validated by suffering.

Solzhenitsyn in his first novel, *The First Circle*, makes one of the political prisoners, Bobynin, say to Abakumov, head of the security police: 'You make a mistake there, Chief. You've taken everything away from me. A man from whom you have taken everything is no longer in your power. He is free all over again.' We hear in those words the echo of an earlier stripping: 'They crucified him and the criminals with him one on his right and the other on his left. Jesus said, "Father, forgive them: they do not know what they are doing." And they divided his clothes among them by casting lots.'

What Jesus demonstrates, what Solzhenitsyn celebrates in his writings, is man's ability to survive as a moral being stripped of all possessions and honour; but purged and purified and lifted up as a man. The heroes of Solzhenitsyn's novels are men who like their author survive at great cost to themselves; but at no cost to others. Beaten down, these men can still say: 'We did not bow down to idols: we did not collaborate with our oppressors: we did not betray our fellow men.'

The inner thrust of Solzhenitsyn's writing is a concern for truth, in the full biblical range of meaning. Not just factual accuracy: truth means also trustworthiness, reliability, integrity. Such is the truth that makes men free, that authenticates itself. We cannot afford not to listen to what such men say to us. We cannot afford not to attend to what God says to us in the arrest, the trial, the crucifixion and the resurrection of Jesus. For these events, more than any other in the world's history, search a man's conscience and make him ask 'By what values am I living my life and to what purpose?'

Against all communications that reduce human beings to the level of animals or robots, there stands the Christian faith, the Christian doctrine, the Christian Church. When will the 'great British public' see the truth of what the Church stands for? When shall we the Church discover how to communicate better than we do to the great British public the truth of what we stand for? We stand for one crucial, central affirmation: that a human being is a being who has to do with God. Only when human persons acknowledge that, will they have the vision and the energy and the grace to become fully human persons in relation to other persons. And this is the real meaning of Christianity.

When did you last ask yourselves what is the real meaning of baptism? When did you last seriously ask yourselves what is the central affirmation of Christianity in face of the fundamental human crisis of the twentieth century? What is it that Christianity really has to say to men and women today? Do you really believe that the central affirmation of Christianity is that a human being is a being who has to do with God and that he can only be genuinely fully human if he lives out his life in this conviction? If you do really believe this, then you will see that baptism is one of the ways in which Christianity makes this affirmation and enables this affirmation to make a difference.

A sacrament works on two levels: it *says* something and it *does* something.

What baptism *says* is that all men and women are children of God. What baptism *does* is to make this claim in connection with this particular person, this particular child who comes to baptism. What baptism *does* is to include this particular person, this particular child within the community of those who live their lives in the conviction that a human being is not a naked ape in a human zoo – not a pawn in somebody else's power game, not just a number in some card index or series of holes punched in a card and entered in the data base of a computer; but a being who has to do with God. Baptism is the spearhead of the Christian attack on all those modern communications that in effect reduce human beings to the level of the higher animals and reject the claims of the transcendent vision and destiny of men as the Christian faith proclaims it.

If this is what baptism is all about, what should we be doing to help people to see this as its meaning? What should we be doing to exalt baptism so that the Christian's affirmation of the true dignity, vocation, and destiny of human persons can become again a rallying point for those of our contemporaries who are dismayed by what they see to be destructive in our present way of life, but do not see in the Church the secret and the power of recovery and restoration of conviction and hope? What should we be doing?

Make a list of the names of those men and women now dead who have touched your life in the past and have helped you to become what you are. All of us have such people in our experience - men and women who have opened our eyes, who have stood with us in a crisis, who have loved us and given us confidence. All Souls' Day is an opportunity to remember and to thank God for all such people. For though they are dead to us in one sense, they are alive to us in another: alive within us for all that we are but would not have been had they not touched our lives and enriched us. I expect we can all say of someone 'If it were not for him, for her, I would not be what I am now'. And occasionally, sadly, we shall use those words not of an influence which has made for our good but an influence that has caused us harm. So perhaps there is lurking resentment or bitterness against someone now dead. If that is so, All Souls' Day gives us a chance to look at the relationship and to ask ourselves if resentment should not now be wiped out by forgiveness.

The healing Christ is the compassionate Christ. And those who allow themselves to meditate on the compassion of Christ are led on to meditate on the compassion of God. For the heart-breaking pains and distresses of humanity raise the most searching questions about the goodness of God. If there is a Reality such as we indicate by this word God, can such a Reality be good and powerful and yet allow all this brokenness and suffering of humanity's history and experience? If God is good and loving and looks upon the world he has allowed to be, surely his heart, if he has a heart, will break. The Christian with the daring of faith points to Christ on the cross and says 'His heart does break'.

Only a Church broken in contrition and penitence, only a Christian broken in contrition and penitence can bring healing to a crippled world. And only when Christians of different traditions and denominations stand side by side and look out towards men and women in their varied needs, only when Christians allow compassion and caring to draw them into action, will they themselves be drawn together into more loving cooperation, and the true unity of the Church find expression. Real unity begins when one Christian of one tradition allows himself to recognise, to acknowledge the Christlike qualities of another Christian of another tradition. Such recognition of kinship, such acknowledgement is more likely to happen in the course of working together in some outside action of help than in any other way. And what action can bring us all to the level of our common humanity more effectively than action related to suffering?

The fact of pain in our experience is so persistent and the questions it raises in our minds so perplexing, that any effort to deepen our understanding of it is likely in some measure to help us to discover how to live with it. For to live with pain is to be alive. Pain is a necessary ingredient in our human experience.

Let this be our starting point – that pain is not a hostile intruder into human experience but a necessary ingredient. An attitude to pain that sees it as an intruder is, I believe, misleading. It is based on a reading of the early chapters of the book of Genesis which treats that story of creation as if it were a historical description of how things began. Perhaps even more it is based on the kind of thinking about the way things began which John Milton universalised and which have become a permanent part of what I might call the folk- theology of many people.

I mean the idea that in the beginning man was happy and innocent and carefree and pain-free in a garden existence until he disobeyed the rules and was driven out of the garden into the unhappy, sinful, anxious, painful experience we call history. This whole sequence of images – Paradise given, Paradise lost, Paradise regained – inevitably leads to the belief that pain is an intruder; that the Creator has blundered; that if we had been God we would have organised things differently. But the Genesis-Miltonic story of Paradise given and Paradise lost is not history. That is not how it happened. In the absence of real knowledge about how it all began, men and women from earliest times have filled in this tantalising gap for themselves by telling stories about how it all began. But you and I, as a result of the research of scientists for the last century or so, are in a different case: we do know much more about the actual way things, animals, persons have developed; even if science can never tell us why there is something and not nothing.

Scientists tell a story about human beginning and human development that we must not ignore; it is vital for our understanding of ourselves. In this story the scientists tell of the long march of everyman from the jungle and the cave to the concrete city and all our present woes. In it pain is seen as a necessary ingredient, a necessary biological warning system which enables survival. Physical pain is a basic human experience which causes us to seek food and warmth and safety and companionship. Pain is a stimulus to seek solutions; pain animates the processes that lead to culture and civilisation. Pain as a fundamental biological mechanism that makes survival and growth possible continues with us on the long march and the long quest.

Modern medical science and skill knows how to relieve us of a great deal of physical pain such as our forefathers had to endure without benefit of analgesics. We must be grateful for that. But physical pain is not the only pain. As we have developed our human sensitivities, our more vulnerable, inner-feeling self experiences pain hurtfully in mind and heart. The human animal has become more self-aware, more capable of feelings of affection and compassion. I mention only pain in the heart at separation whether by distance or by death; pain of loneliness, anxiety, betrayal, doubt; pain of growing old, of hard circumstances and uncertainty, of a sense of meaninglessness. Pain in mind and heart are our continuing experience, part of the givenness of being alive and human. The more we love, the more vulnerable we become. Pain so considered is no blunder of the Creator, no alien intruder but a permanent resident in the house. Sometimes the pain we experience is the direct consequence of our own foolishness and blindness; sometimes of our deliberate fault. God allows us to suffer the consequences. I do not understand those who speak as if God directly sends pain as punishment for wrongdoing.

Because an individual is a single organism with body, mind and spirit inter-penetrating each other, body affects mind and mind affects body. But our precious gift is spirit. Our spirit fortified by the Holy Spirit has the power when truly developed to use all pain in such a way that it transforms it from a source of anger, resentment, or self-pity into an energy making for deeper understanding, deeper compassion, deeper love.

The *new* thing in this world of mankind's evolving history, the 'intruder' if you like, is not pain but love – the kind of loving of which Christ spoke when he said 'A new commandment I give you, that you love one another'. For this Christ-love is a power of love that can take the evil out of situations and transform it into its opposite. What else is the Word of the Cross if not this? It has been said of Jesus that he learned obedience by the things he suffered. Pain is changed in the crucible of love by Christ's strange alchemy. Love is the divine intruder into the evolving process, but an intruder still unrecognised by many; for some of the time unrecognised by all of us. But to those who admit the divine intruder into their soul, love creates good and healing relationships.

Of all the reasons why the claims of Christianity deserve to be taken seriously, the reason that for me has always been the most persuasive is the fact that Christianity takes pain seriously; that at its centre is the sign of suffering love transfiguring the pain; that the healing it offers comes from the hands of a wounded healer. 'He saved others: himself he could not save.' Christ the pain-bearer enables us to bear pain so that for us as for him it makes for an increase of the world's resources of love.

If pain is so central to all our experience in one form or another; if pain can become for each of us either an irritant making for our misery and the misery of others, or else a power making for increased goodness and love; then learning how to deal with pain, our own pain and other people's pain, would seem to be very near the centre of what most warrants our best attention as Christians and our continuing concern.

What does it mean to be risen with Christ? What are the distinguishing marks of a man or a woman who is risen with Christ? The phrase is not to be taken literally as a physical parallel to the death and resurrection of Christ. The phrase, like so many other Christan phrases, is a metaphor; the meaning is a transferred meaning; the meaning is transferred from a single event in time to something capable of being experienced and expressed at all times, by each and every individual. 'To be risen' requires a previous 'to be dead' – or rather a continual dying and continual rising. The words speak of something interior to each person: a change of values, attitudes and expectations finding expression in new patterns of behaviour, of actual manner of life.

What then are the distinguishing marks of a person who is risen with Christ? A new gratitude and a new generosity. Gratitude and generosity are words which speak of a fundamental change in the depths of the soul from self-centredness and selfishness and self-pity and possessiveness and all kinds of meanness. I speak of the change from being shut in to being opened out. 'Shut-inness' is the condition we call death – the self shut in upon itself in a tomb of its own choosing. 'Open-outness' is the condition we call being raised from death – the self looking out on the world with eyes open to other people; and so a self seeing itself in the truth of its condition. To see the truth about one's condition is to see oneself and all others with the eyes of Christ. To be risen with Christ, then, means – along with much else – to be growing in gratitude for all we have received from others; to be growing in generosity towards all others so that they may be enriched by what they receive from our giving of ourselves. The whole point about taking care about our inner attitudes is that we shall be set free from the death of negative states of mind and set free for the new life of positive states of mind. We have to become what we shall have to give. Christianity is all about this: self-becoming for self-giving. This is a dying and a rising – a dying to the destructive attitudes of selfishness and greed; a rising to the creative attitudes of gratitude and generosity. 'Freely you have received; freely give.'

Anyone who speaks to others about prayer is inevitably speaking also to himself. He speaks to some extent out of his own experience, to some extent out of the experience of others who have taught him what he knows, by spoken or by written word and by example; but to a great extent he speaks to himself as one of the audience whom he is addressing. For anyone who speaks to others about prayer is himself in need of encouragement, of full understanding and of a practice more nearly related to the principles on which he dares to speak.

When we pray to God using words of gratitude or penitence, of adoration or anguish, we are not speaking to ourselves – we are speaking to God. But we are also hearers of what we say; and what we hear is ourselves talking to God. As it were, we overhear our heart voicing its fears and its hopes, its doubts and its longings. We learn to pray by praying. By praying we do something to ourselves. This is not the reason we pray: it is a kind of by-product of praying, but it is important for our self-understanding, our self-estimation. It helps us to be real, to be honest about our inner selves. The more we grow through prayer in awareness of God, as presence, as claim, as enabling grace, so do we grow in awareness of ourself – as we are and as we desire to be. This is part of the reciprocity of prayer: we give and we receive. We acknowledge and we assimilate what we acknowledge. As the writer of the medieval treatise *The Cloud of Unknowing* says in quaint but memorable words: 'Therefore swink and sweat in all that thou canst and mayest for to get thee a true knowing and a feeling of thyself as thou art, for then I trow that, soon after that, thou shalt have a true knowing and a feeling of God as he is.'

To pray is to give ourselves the opportunity to become more aware of God and in that awareness to respond to him. Prayer is a kind of song in the heart, a song of response from one who has reflected on the wonder that he is loved by God in spite of what he has come to know about himself – and from that reflection strives to offer a better love to God.

I hope that none of you is without some experience of human love, some feeling of affection for another. Dr Jack Dominian has written: 'Human love is an instrument we can use to explore the mystery of divine love.' What does it mean to love God? Cardinal Hume has put it like this: 'If I have experienced love or affection for others, I can comprehend dimly, inadequately, incompletely, not so much what God should mean to me, but what I mean to God.'

I suppose I always knew that I meant a great deal to my mother. But I only really began to know the depth of that love while I was with her during the last weeks of her diminishment into death. Similarly, in whatever relationship you and I experience love, either in giving to another or receiving from another, we can, if we will, begin to discern in this something of what each of us means to God. If I love a particular person very much and that person means much to me, I have here a window opening on to the relationship in which I stand with God. 'We only love God', St John tells us, 'because God first loved us.'

Spiritual writers tell us that it is more important to love God than to know him. At the heart of prayer is desire, a simple longing to respond to a love which was first offered to us, a greater desire for God, even if our understanding seems to grow not at all.

There is a genuine and important place for intellect and thought in religion, because people do ask intellectual questions. Theology is a necessary activity within the Christian community. But prayer is an exercise in which the mind is held in the heart, and it is the longings and desires of the heart that seek expression in prayer. We tend to be shy of letting ourselves go, of letting our feelings out. But our feelings matter and need outlet. Prayer is one outlet for our deepest feelings. Prayer is a response from the depths of our being. St Teresa of Avila asked of a person who was searching for God with her mind alone: 'Why do you look for God here, why do you look there? God is within you.' As the Psalmist says: 'Commune with your own heart and be still'; 'Be still and know that I am God.'

Words like 'still', 'silence', 'waiting', 'contemplating' are important words to indicate the kind of praying of which I am trying to speak. Artists know what it means to be still, to be silent, to wait, to contemplate. Often, too, you can observe these qualities in small children absorbed in their play. But how often adults are restless, talkative, unhappy unless they are doing something, so busy that they do not see what is really there. Of course there is a place for activity, we must fulfil the duties of our state of life, the Martha syndrome; but there is also a place for comtemplation, the Mary syndrome. The contemplative person can be active without anxiety, without hurry, without endless chatter. Have you ever been in an engine room where there is a great dynamo generating electricity – whirling around at high speed and yet so beautifully made that what strikes you is the peace and the quiet rather than the speed?

Most of us are called to be active-contemplatives, the Martha-Mary emphasis. Our prayer is to be contemplative so that from within the serenity and peace it engenders we can get on with what is required of us, do what has to be done, without fret and without anxiety. There are a few who are called to be contemplative-actives, the Mary-Martha emphasis. Sometimes these are individual persons with a special calling to the prayer of quiet, in communities whose ordered life of prayer gives shape to their day and the necessary activities are fitted in between the times of prayer. The essential element in a life of contemplation is looking towards God, the giving back of our whole being to God who is the source of our being. Such prayer develops by penetrating more deeply, in the Spirit, into the hidden Mystery of Christ.

What this kind of prayer is like we can discover by reading the writings of St Teresa of Avila or St John of the Cross. St John of the Cross expressed his love in poems. If you did not know the author you might read the poems and think of them as belonging to the category of human love poems – like the love poems in that Old Testament book we call The Song of Songs. But for St Bernard of Clairvaux and others, the erotic poetry of The Song of Songs has been interpreted as the longing of the soul in love-response to God. Once again as Dr Dominian said, 'Human love is an instrument we can use to explore the mystery of divine love.'

The Celtic element in our northern race is not without passion and the song in the heart. Even if we find this warmer, more feeling, more effusive devotion not natural to our temperament, I believe we impoverish our religious response if there is no such warmth in our devotion. Something of this element of a feeling devotion comes through some of our well-known hymns – especially those from writers like Watts and Wesley. We should not be afraid of such prayer of the heart; nor think of loving God in terms only of deliberate choice, will, duty. Let contemplation of the reality of God's love for us awaken within us a warm, passionate response. The essence of religion is adoration.

We must pray as we can and not press ourselves into kinds of prayer that do not suit us. What suits one person will not suit another. Each of us participates as we can in the public worship of the Church; each of us has his and her own way of praying in private. But in all our praying there needs to be something of the song in the heart, something of the warmth of devotion, something of the element of adoration.

I believe that the sheer existence of religious communities committed to prayer and contemplation rather than the world of welfare and active charity – Mary communities rather than Martha communities – is of the utmost importance to the whole Church. If you like to put it so, it exaggerates an emphasis on prayer and thereby keeps prayer securely at the centre of the Church's life and provides places of silence into which the more active ones among us can from time to time go for renewal of prayer in quiet and silence – a private retreat or a retreat made in company with others. We draw strength and encouragement for contemplative prayer on our own journey, from the knowledge of those men and women whose self-offering of love to Divine Love takes this form of total commitment.

Within our Anglican Church such houses of contemplative prayer as Fairacres in Oxford and West Malling in Kent are centres which radiate the love of God into many lives of those who are for a short while drawn into the continuing life of contemplation which is their vocation and discipline. What we are talking about when we speak of the prayer of contemplation is enabling the action of God in a person's life to be unhindered, to be set free to do its work. For this to happen, and it can and surely is meant to happen in all our lives, we have to make leisure for God. In order that God shall be free to act in us and through us in love to others all of the time, we have to secure some of the time for the leisure of prayer, the freedom from all other demands. By waiting still upon God in silent prayer, adoration, openness, we may gradually grow into people in whose active lives the steady undercurrent is generated by a heart always turned to God, always seeking God, always seeing whatever happens as another occasion for cooperating with God in that situation.

And what is all this if not the working out in practice of the inner power of the Lord's Prayer.

Our Father, who art in heaven,
Hallowed be thy name,
Thy kingdom come,
Thy will be done – in me.

Overheard in the Close on Friday. A small boy sitting on the wall gazing at the Cathedral, hugging his small dog and wishing to turn the dog's attention in the same direction. But small dog was not attentive to his master's voice: proximity of a cat was disturbing dog's attention. Small master's voice more severe now: 'You'll be able to see hundreds more cats – but you'll never see the Cathedral again.'

An echo perhaps of small boy's parents struggling to win small boy's attention to the things that matter; an echo perhaps of another Master's voice, 'Seek ye first the kingdom of God and his righteousness.'

What parent, what teacher, what preacher is there who does

not understand small boy's exasperation? Nothing is more difficult than to win undivided and undistracted attention of an audience to the matter in hand. What matters most is not always what is most immediately attractive. To pay attention is, as the phrase suggests, a costly activity. But to pay attention to the things that most matter is the urging of the Master's voice in the Gospels. To pray is to pay attention to what matters most: and prayer as we all discover is a costly activity and not what is most immediately attractive.

We each need to explore with considerable urgency what constitutes a true Christian seriousness. Whatever else belongs to a true Christian seriousness, at least it belongs that we should pay attention to both the signals of doom and the symbols of hope. Of the energies that are making for destruction none of us should be ignorant; and each of us should find some way of adding our support to one or other of the agencies of hope. Every individual counts and every voice adds to the volume of protest and of persuasion. If you feel that the most you can do is so small in face of what needs to be done, do not for that reason hold back. None of us can do more than we can; but not to do even the little we can is betrayal.

To be better informed is something we can all do.

To keep watch on the things we say is something we can all do.

To become involved in one activity which is geared to conserve rather than to destroy is something we can all do.

To determine to take our life-stand by faith and choice within the creative and re-creative energies of God is something we can all do.

To take the life-offering, life-enhancing spirit of the Eucharist out from this Cathedral into all our relationships is something we can all do.

Let every Christian be seen as a walking symbol of hope among all the signals and symptoms of doom. Reflect on the Gospel story as you go about your daily business: 'When Jesus was come near, he beheld the city and wept over it, saying, "If thou hadst known, even thou, at least in this thy day, the things which belong unto thy peace! but now they are hid from thine eye."'

So what did he do? Did he despair? He did what he could. He cleansed the temple of its trivialities and its misuse – and he taught daily. Like the small boy with his dog, he urged all he could persuade to listen, to pay attention to the things that really matter. Protest and persuasion were the methods Christ used; and they should be ours.

It is for our own good as well as for the good of others that we need to come to terms with that whole area of our experience that is indicated by the words 'alone', 'lonely', 'loneliness', 'solitude'. These words do not all speak of an identical experience. Solitude and loneliness do not indicate the same emotion.

Solitude is a dimension of the human condition, one of the facts of being human. Loneliness is a dimension of the human experience – of human emotion – which some feel more acutely than others, and some suffer from more continuously than others. It is by coming to terms with our essential human condition of solitude that we shall be better able to cope with our human experience – our human feeling of loneliness. For the sake of others as well as for our own sake it is all important to understand, acknowledge, accept our condition of solitude; and to learn how to handle, live with, and transpose our feelings of loneliness.

There is one sentence of supreme significance in St John's marvellous Chapter 17 when he presents Christ in an extended prayer to the Father. Christ in this prayer says: 'For their sakes I consecrate myself.'

Years of meditation will never take us to the full inwardness of this affirmation. But put it into common speech, it means in a general way: 'For the sake of others I will endeavour to reach a truly godward orientation of my own inner self.'

The way we are with others – the way other people find us to be – is all bound up with the way we are with ourselves. And the way we are with ourselves is all bound up with the way we are with God. And the way we are with God is all bound up with the way we are with others. And at the heart of this triangle of relationships is our condition of solitude and our experience of loneliness.

If you will sometime sit in the Trinity Chapel and contemplate the triangle of light reaching out from the apex of the cross, such a meditation will take you more deeply into the essentially Christian understanding of what is involved in the way we are with God – transfiguring the way we are with ourselves and therefore, the way we are with others.

The sheer physical fact of aloneness is sometimes aggravated by circumstances. I remember how Gonville ffrench-Beytagh, one time Dean of the Cathedral in Johannesburg, described the experience of being arrested by the South African police and the overwhelming sense of being alone when the cell door was banged and locked.

The accidents of circumstance that aggravate our aloneness as a fact can therefore also increase our feeling of loneliness. And it is, I expect, the feeling of loneliness rather than the fact of aloneness that leads some people to seek relief from the pain by methods that in the event fail to relieve the pain. There are the tranquillisers, there is alcohol, there is sexual stimulation which is quite other than the sacramental intercourse of a true loving relationship; there is the constant telephoning of long-suffering friends. But none of these escape routes from the pain of loneliness goes to the root of the trouble. None of these escape routes sets us free from that most debilitating of all inner states – indulgence in self-pity. Our ability to live with feelings of loneliness is all bound up with our understanding and acceptance of our essential solitude as human beings.

Solitude is an inescapable truth of our human condition. Sincere friendships can for a time diminish our consciousness of our essential solitude. But no friend can remove those moments of awareness that come upon us as we lie awake at night, or if we have a really difficult decision to make, or when we are very ill. No friend can be ill for us. No friend can relieve us of the necessity to die. And when we die – we die alone even if we are supported by friends.

To face the fact of our essential solitude; to face the anguish which this sense of our essential solitude sometimes causes us; to face the inevitable death that one day we each must die; to face the fact and acknowledge that this is the way things really are for us; to take in this unpalatable truth and not try to push it away; *this* I believe is a mark of Christian maturity and the way to inner freedom. Do this and you will find it a source of inner strength for coping with the accidents of circumstance that bereave us of someone dearly beloved or deprive us of some objective dearly desired. We shall find ourselves better able to cope with the anguish of loneliness.

But how shall we reach such inner maturity of soul except by faith and prayer? For prayer is both a work we do and a work God does within us if we give God the opportunity by laying our wounds open to him.

So in our middle years when so much is demanded of us by our responsibilities, when we are wearied by inescapable activity, we shall do well to seek more solitude and to respect the solitude of others. A wise writer once said that husband and wife should be guardians of each other's solitude. Certainly parents should guard the solitude of their children. For to respect and guard our own and other people's solitude is to acknowledge our individual uniqueness and the unique growth we each must achieve. Chosen solitude and chosen prayer enables us really to inhabit the house of our inner self; to know who we are; to know who others are; to know the world in which we are set to live; to know God as the loving presence in whom we live and move and have our being.

What is special about Jesus? One element in the answer is the power of the Jesus story to evoke in every century and in every nation a continuing interest, a continuing enquiry, a continuing rejection, a continuing acceptance. A second element in the answer is the capacity of the Jesus story to latch on to the imagination of different individuals in different ways. Each person responds to his or her own vision of Jesus. There is a fascinating paradox in all this. There was only one Jesus; but there are as many Jesuses as there are individuals who respond to him. My Jesus is not your Jesus. If each of us were to say exactly who Jesus is for himself, for herself, we would each speak of the one and the same historical Jesus, but we would each speak of a different Jesus, a Jesus of our own imagining, a Jesus who means this to me and that to you. This has always been so.

We have three written documents which tell the Jesus story. All these were written within thirty or forty years of the events that culminated in his crucifixion and the emergence of the community of his resurrection. But each of these three portraits of the one and the same Jesus is a distinctive portrait in the sort of way that three different artists today would produce three distinctive portraits of the same sitter. The fourth written document – later in time and known by the name of John – paints the Jesus story and presents the person of Jesus in an even more contrasting fashion. All four Gospel writers give us the same Jesus and a different Jesus – Jesus as he has become through the mesh and filter of each writer's imagination and received tradition and personal response. Each writer gives his own answer to the question, 'What's special about Jesus?' The same is true of other New Testament writers: Paul, James, the author of the Hebrews.

What then is special? We have identified two elements so far. First, his capacity to attract, to hold the interest, to raise questions in the mind and stimulate the imagination of men and women in every century and in every continent. Secondly, his capacity to evoke an individual response from each individual person so that we can say that each such person, whether accepting or rejecting, has a Jesus who is his own.

We can now add a third ingredient to our preliminary answer. He makes a difference to the inner thinking of everyone who takes him seriously and opens his imagination and his heart to the story that has Jesus at its centre. There is something in this story for everybody. It acts like a mirror and it acts like a window.

It acts like a mirror in so far as it causes us to take a new view of ourselves. We see ourselves in a new light. In certain ways what we see is painful: it makes us ashamed; it makes us want to discard certain attitudes, certain aims, and adopt new aims and different attitudes. In other aspects the mirror-like element in the story is reassuring. It strengthens our confidence in the desirability of certain other aims and certain other attitudes.

But the Jesus story acts also like a window opening on a larger world of possibilities. We see a different sort of future for ourselves and for others, a different quality of relationships, a deeper level of meaning. We see fresh areas of personal growth, new openings for service, awakening awareness of human need, human pain, human anguish. Jesus is a window into the heart of men and women. Jesus is a window into the heart of God.

If this were not so, if what is special about Jesus were not seen as special for us now, if Jesus did not in some way capture our attention now, our desire now, opening up for us a new view of ourselves, a new vision of our possibilities of growth and of service, it is inconceivable that anyone now would be wanting to spend time trying to get to know Jesus as he was – as he was experienced by those who were his first friends and his first enemies in the Palestine of all those centuries ago. But it is a fact of our time that many men and women are concerned to understand who Jesus was just because they find in what they know of him now something that speaks with a deeply felt personal human need. What can we know of this man who gets under our skin as no other man does?

As we ask to know more about Jesus as he was – this man who told his stories and won his friends and provoked his enemies – we enter an area which has occupied many able Christian minds for nearly 2,000 years and has raised all kinds of difficult questions for which there are no clear and final answers.

We have the four written Gospel portraits, but they are not photographs. Even if we had a documentary film of those first-century events we know that a documentary film is edited: we are shown what the photographer and what the editor choose to show us. We have no tape recordings of Jesus actually speaking; no court-writers' account of the trial of Jesus in *The Times* next day. The only contact we have with Jesus the historical man is contact through documents which by their very nature are interpretations, not recordings. The Gospel portraits are interpretations of Jesus the man based on experience of Jesus within the group of his friends after he had been crucified and buried. After-death experience was what caused them to think differently about what they remembered of what he said and did before he died. The only Jesus we can reach historically is a remembered and interpreted Jesus by a company of men and women who were gripped by a conviction about what was special about him, which took hold of them after all the events which led up to his death.

These writers wrote to persuade others of the truth they saw in Jesus. They wrote to communicate to others what they believed to be special about Jesus – special in their own experience and in the experience of the ever-growing communities of Christians in that ancient world. But the words, the phrases, the expressions they used in order to express what they found to be special about Jesus is a language which is strange to our twentieth-century ears. What can we make of these words and phrases?

Yet just how important is it for our Christian discipleship today that we cannot know in more exact detail who Jesus was? Do we really need to know for certain whether everything described in the Gospels happened like that? Do we really need to know for certain whether everything Jesus is reported as having said was actually said by him and in those words?

This is an area of problem for many thinking Christians, and for many others who would like to be counted among the Christians but do not know how with integrity to handle the strangeness of certain central elements in the Jesus story as it has come down to us. If the Gospels do not have the kind of authority that we would acknowledge in a historical document, contemporary with the events and written to give an accurate account, does that matter? Does faith in Christ require that kind of knowledge of the historical Jesus? Or does faith depend rather on the fact that Jesus and the events that happened in connection with Jesus have for nearly 2,000 years been found to act as a mirror and as a window which have produced results which authenticate the truth that is Christ Jesus as a truth of far greater significance than any ancient contemporary document by itself could ever provide?

My own faith is grounded on the reality of Jesus Christ as a continuing centre of creative energy now as then, a reality to which the Gospels direct our attention in a way that does not depend on their being documents whose historical validity in all detail or indeed in the intention of their writers is to be regarded as the ground of their authority. What is special about Jesus is a far more mysterious and a far more marvellous reality than that of a man who once upon a time lived and died in Galilee and Jerusalem.

For many human beings the past is past and to be discarded and forgotten like old socks. What matters is what is now, the latest model. I think this state of mind is of recent origin: it belongs to the age of the machine. A machine that no longer works, such as a watch that is beyond repair, is good for nothing and to be thrown away. Go round any farm buildings and you will see discarded machinery. And there was that American visitor recently who said we ought to sell Magna Carta and build a new Cathedral because this one's 'kind of old-fashioned'.

Like much modern thinking this is superficial. The past does matter. The past is prologue to the present; and themes spoken in the prologue of a book or a play are themes worked out in the following acts and pages. What could be more old-fashioned than Dickens's *Christmas Carol*? And yet this old story has its present power and meaning. For while the outward circumstances of our human existence may change (the Welfare State today is very different from the contrast between wealth and poverty in Dickens's day) we as human beings change very little across the centuries. The self-centred miser and the generous poor are with us still and within us still. And the story of Jesus, the things his friends remembered about him, the stories he himself told, the things he said to individuals, all that he suffered, this acts as powerfully today as it ever did – a mirror in which we see ourselves in a new light, a window through which we see a different landscape, a different vision of what human life can be.

If we press our question, 'What is it that makes Jesus so special?' and ask who therefore Jesus is, we are asking the same question that men and women were asking twenty centuries ago, questions they wrestled with in those written documents we call the New Testament, questions that have engaged some of the best intellects of all the years and still provoke controversy within the Christian community today. The names of Küng and Schillebeeckx, of Robinson and Cupitt echo the names of Nestorius and Arius and Athanasius and Cyril who wrestled long ago with this same question. What is the secret of this enigmatic man? Who is he?

The Jewish establishment of those far-off times, the Jewish authorities, said of Jesus: 'He's an impostor. He's a blasphemer. He makes claims to forgive sins; and that power belongs to Yahweh alone. Away with this man. Crucify him.' But the common people we are told heard Jesus gladly, and the temple guards sent to arrest him came back empty-handed. 'We've never heard anyone speak as this man speaks.' And in another place: 'He speaks with authority.' It was this inner authority of Jesus that seems to have drawn some people to him and to have alienated others. But what created the community of his resurrection, the community of friends and followers who so quickly spread and won new adherents? What raised the question 'What is special about Jesus?' was their overwhelming sense after his crucifixion that he was present with them and within them as the animating spirit of their new experience of an inner freedom, joy, purpose, mission. So the search began for an answer to the question 'Who is this man?' And being Jews and being believers in Yahweh and being brought up in a religious tradition that was essentially forward-looking and expecting God to intervene and inaugurate a new age, what else could they have concluded but that the new age had come and that Jesus was God's agent, God's Messiah. They answered their question about what is special about Jesus by casting him in the role of the expected deliverer. So they called him Messiah, Son of David, Christ, Son of Man, he who should come, Son of God.

These titles which were familiar within the Jewish community were unfamiliar among the Gentiles – the Greeks and Romans of the wider world within which the Jews lived. And so the search went on to find ways of speaking about Jesus to people who had a different religious and cultural background. For good or ill – I have never convinced myself which – the debate was taken up by the theologians and philosophers who wanted to define too much, too precisely. They spoke of abstract entities like 'humanity', 'divinity'. How, they asked, could God become man without ceasing to be God? How could a man be God without ceasing to be a man?

Those Christian creeds that we still say, those Christian canticles like the Te Deum that we still sing, can only be understood by us in our yet again so different world of the twentieth century if we understand them as agreed, historically conditioned statements coming at the end of centuries of debate in a cultural setting not our own. But in saying the Creed today we proclaim our identity with, our continuity with, those earlier generations of the Christian family. We proclaim that we stand in relation to Jesus where they stood, even if their way of saying what is special about Jesus is for us full of problems.

Take the title 'Son of God'. It meant one thing to an ancient Jew, a different thing to an ancient Greek. But to both it was an experience cast in the form of a metaphor. '*Son*-language' like '*Father*-language' is human language. To speak of the ultimate reality, to speak of God as Father is to transfer the word from its human biological meaning to help us to cope with the inexpressible mystery of God, and Christians were encouraged to speak of God as Father because that was how Jesus spoke of God and spoke to God. But when they went on to speak of Jesus as Son of God they were not saying something biological as I should be meaning if I spoke of myself as my human father's son. To use of God the word 'Father', to use of Jesus the word 'Son', is not to say something biological but to say something metaphorical, to speak of a mysterious relationship by likening it to a relationship within our experience.

So for us to say that Jesus is the Son of God is to say that the relationship between God and Jesus has a closeness like that of the relationship between a human father and his son when that relationship is one of likeness of personality, of warmth of feeling, of reciprocity of trust. When Jesus is reported as saying 'He who has seen me has seen the Father', that word at least means: 'If you see how I speak of the Father and relate to the Father, you will understand what kind of a Father God is.' So relationship in terms of closeness, trust, obedience, and love is what is being spoken of when we speak of Jesus as Son of God, rather than something genetic or something which calls in question the reality of Jesus as a human person knowing the reality of choice and of pain.

Our modern difficulty, however, is made greater by the fact that nowadays we have less clear ideas of what we mean when we speak of God. To say that what is special about Jesus is that he is uniquely Son of God does not exactly illuminate the question for somebody who then asks 'But what are you speaking of when you use this word God?'

To recognise the uniqueness of Jesus is one thing; to find ways of speaking about that uniqueness is another; and yet another thing is it to interpret the uniqueness of Jesus in terms of the meaning of being alive and being human in this world. The mystery of our being, the mystery of our meaning as human beings eludes verbal analysis and verbal description. Nonetheless for Christian faith the question 'What is special about Jesus?' is all bound up with the mystery of being alive and being human in this world – the mystery that is you and me. And Christians are people who find themselves unable to interpret the mystery of being alive and being human except in terms of that other mystery for which our indicator word is 'God'.

What is special about Jesus is that he for us uniquely discloses the hidden reality which is the ultimate dimension of the life we are all living – he discloses it as a relationship of trust, of faith, of prayer, of obedience to the point of death on the cross. The face of Jesus is for us 'the human face of God'.

We are much more aware nowadays than were our forefathers of other world religions with their vast followings. Until recently we could forget them: they were distant, they lived in foreign parts. Now more and more Muslims and Hindus and Buddhists are living in Britain, and the media bring religious world news into our homes. Also we are aware of many men and women who would not call themselves Christians or Churchmen, who seem to have absorbed much of the Christian attitude towards those who are poor, disabled, unjustly treated: honest people who care for their neighbours. They often canvass causes with which we as Christians find ourselves in sympathy and support, and with an enthusiasm we do not always emulate. There is a kind of diffused Christian humanism whose adherents have never really examined the assumptions on which they choose what they will do and value what they value. There is a pervasive presence and influence of Jesus that colours human lives well beyond the boundaries of anything that could be called membership of the Church or commitment to Christ.

These humanists with discernible Christian characteristics in their motivation are often baffled by what seems to be required of them if they were to embrace full Christian faith. They do not understand our language, they see no point in our worship. The members of other world religions challenge us to explain on what grounds we make such claims as we seem to make for the uniqueness of Jesus. What is so special about Jesus that makes him different from other religious teachers such as Buddha and Mohammed? On what grounds do we make universal claims for him?

The story that is told about Jesus, our Christian story, all the stories Jesus himself told that are retold in our Christian story, are quite different from the story told about Mohammed or about Buddha, quite different from the stories told by other great religious innovators. Each of the great world religions explores the deeper dimensions of human experience: that is what they have in common. But what they each offer as an interpretation of the meaning of the human mystery is distinct and different. There are all kinds of reasons for these distinctive differences – historical, cultural, linguistic, philosophical. They cannot be amalgamated as if they were just variations on the same theme. Each must be allowed to stand in its own right, and a choice has to be made between them. From time to time there are a few people who discard one and adopt another, but for the most part people remain where they are in their distinct and different ways of speaking about the meaning and mystery of human life. So on what grounds does anyone opt for Jesus? Most people who opt for Jesus do so without going into a deep examination of alternatives. They are brought up within the Christian community and are more or less influenced by its style of life. There are also those who are brought into the community of Christian faith from choice because they are attracted by the quality of life of some individual or of some group; and choose these in preference to their own isolation, or despair, or bewilderment. Many, many more live on the fringes of the Christian community, and the Christian faith, uncommitted but not opposed; more for it than against it. I expect this has always been the case for large numbers of British people. But this diffused Christianity in the nation at large will become less influential in sustaining even basic human rights and honesty and ordinary human caring unless there is always a sufficient number of people who allow their lives to be deeply influenced by the teaching of Jesus, by learning from him how to live by faith, by prayer, by hope and by self-giving love.

This man from the past is remembered now and loved now within communities of his friends all over the world. He influences our imagination now, and liberates people now from false values and sets them free now for more creative living because the Church today in its life and worship activates the long memory. The memory is contained in documents that are read week by week and day by day; it is activated by preaching, by prayer and, above all, by the drama of the Eucharist. For in the Eucharist we do more than activate a memory of long-past events: we call them out of the past into the present so that they are real influences now, not just remembered influences of what happened to people who knew Jesus long ago. We enter into these things concerning Jesus as true always, communicating what is true today and will be true tomorrow. This activating of the memory in the long-continuing communities of faith has a transforming, liberating, life-enhancing effect on those who enter into the central radiance. What is special about Jesus is that he is the central radiance of the continuing experience, evoking response and energising love. He offers us not only a new vision of what our own lives can become, he is also the source of new energy for living our lives in response to this different vision. This is what I understand to be the truth of the Christian claims about his resurrection after crucifixion. What happened after his death was the energising of a community of transformed and transforming men and women who understood what was happening to them owing to his continuing presence with them and within them. The further evidence of his being a radiance of new energy for living is the evidence of the quality of life of many of our contemporaries today who in faith have opened mind and heart to his teaching and his person. Quality of life authenticates the claims of faith.

Is it surprising that all down the centuries Christians have said of the living Jesus that he cannot be contained within categories of the merely human, that he can only be understood as a presence within the human of a radiance and a grace that comes into history from beyond history? To say 'But he is Son of God' is to mean by that phrase that in him uniquely we see what it means for a man to be so open to God that God is able to disclose his being and his love in a human, historical life. In Jesus we see what God is and what God desires us to become. In Jesus we see what a true man is and what kind of a man we are each invited to become. Jesus is a window through which we see into the heart of God, a mirror in which we see into the true condition of our own hearts, a radiance which will light up our own eyes and dispel the darkness of our usual selfishness by transforming us into centres of love such as he is, that radiate the love of God in the neighbourhood of our normal relationships. All this evidence and experience makes us convinced that what Paul said about Jesus all those centuries ago is true for us today – God was in Christ reconciling the world to himself.

There is no more fundamental statement about the human condition and the human experience than these words in the ancient Genesis story of how it all began, where it is said: 'So God created man in his own image, in the image of God he created him; male and female he created them.'

Gender is our word for this distinction within the unity of our human nature. He and she. He and she share in a common humanity, but he and she are complementary opposites. Only when these opposites come together and complement each other can life be procreated. The ancient Genesis story says: 'Therefore a man leaves his father and mother and cleaves to his wife and they become one flesh.'

One flesh, yes, but separate persons, different genders, male and female, a reciprocity of qualities we identify as feminine and of qualities we identify as masculine. The physical, sexual differences enable the coming together for the procreation of life. But there are other differences more profound than biological – the differences of maleness and femaleness. These qualities are hard to define with exactness: some women have certain marked masculine characteristics and some men have certain marked feminine characteristics.

These differences of psychology are linked with the biological differences, for in the shared role of procreators and parents the role of the mother is necessarily different from the role of the father. The upbringing of children to manhood and womanhood is fundamentally affected by the differing influence of father and of mother, affected therefore by the absence of father or mother as a result of death or divorce. The characteristics of the two sexes are interdependent and complementary.

What havoc in the course of the centuries human society has made of this interdependence, this complementarity, this reciprocity. Irrelevant attitudes of superiority and inferiority have fouled the nest. Differences of role have been corrupted into differences of status. For in the earliest times it was the need of the mother and the children which required the father to be the hunter. Her immobility caused his adventurousness, her sense of the particular stimulated his sense of the general, her instinct required his logic. Feminine receptivity is served by masculine assertiveness. The sexes and their characteristic strengths were from the start interdependent and remain so.

In the course of history this reciprocity and recognition of being complementary has led to a lopsided pattern of relationship, and generally a male-dominated style of social and political organisation – and frequently to a relationship between male and female which is not truly complementary with an 'e', nor complimentary with an 'i'. Men themselves have had to pay a high price in human loss by developing a dominant and over-cerebral style. The stiff-upper-lip idea of manhood has caused men to cover up their anxieties and vulnerabilities – especially from other men. Undemonstrativeness in turn can sap the sources of feeling. Even Achilles sometimes wept.

With all the changes of recent years by means of education and more opportunities for women to enter professions and trades, there has inevitably grown a greater feminine assertiveness and independence, and the attempt to redress the balance has still further strengthened the over-masculine character of modern consciousness and of modern society. 'Women's Lib', in its efforts to redress the balance by making women more like men, is making for an even more dangerous predominance of masculine characteristics, and an even more dangerous diminishment of the essential feminine characteristics which have been diminished already by male social and political dominance.

A mother's place is no more in the home than a father's place is in the home: *both* belong in the home, fulfilling their reciprocal roles. And already that understanding and that practice is far more developed in many homes today than was the case when I was a child. One of the many splendid qualities of large numbers of younger husbands and wives is their acknowledgement and exploration of reciprocal activities within the family. Whoever it was who invented the supermarket did a magnificent service in the direction of developing shared responsibilities in the family. Many more husbands are happy to do the shopping in a supermarket than would ever be happy to shop around in separate butchers and bakers and grocery stores. But family life is not for all.

There are many men and many women who are not married, not fathers and mothers; and many mothers are widowed and many fathers are widowed. What I am trying to say about maleness and femaleness has to do with society at large – with men and women in themselves, in their self-knowledge, in their consciousness, in their relationships. I am talking about the need for new understandings in male-minds and female-minds, a new consciousness of what it means to be a woman, of what it means to be a man. I am wanting to get out of all our minds the ideas of male superiority and female inferiority. I am primarily talking about what is in our minds, in our inherited thinking about male and female. I am urging a new consciousness. In our centuries-long, male-dominated consciousness I am urging a rediscovery of characteristics which are feminine characteristics of thought and outlook and feeling. I believe that something of the maternal orientation is essential in our masculine consciousness if we are ever to get out of the mess we are making of social and political life and get into a pattern of relationships that is more creative and less destructive of true human values and true human qualities.

Read Luke's presentation of Jesus and you hardly find ma e assertiveness, masculine pride, machismo; nor a man who is less than masculine in his inner strength. Yet you find in Jesus, along with masculine characteristics, many other characteristics we would call feminine. Feminine is not the same word as effeminate. There is nothing effeminate about Jesus. What you find in Jesus the man is a marvellous blend and balance of masculine and feminine characteristics.

Or read some of the wise thinkers of antiquity. Aristotle, Aquinas, Dante stress that the masculine and the feminine must be harmoniously combined to fashion a view of reality that is not distorted. Shakespeare, Donne, Goethe, Blake, each in his own way holds the masculine and the feminine, the objective and the imaginative, the logical and the sensitive together. Things go wrong when either masculine or feminine characteristics achieve dominance.

The spirit of the masculine intellect is probing the secrets of nature and the benefits of the resulting science and technology are great. But let that intellect dominate and you have the predicament we are in - science and technology getting out of control and capable of destroying life altogether. The masculine will destroy us unless it is balanced by the feminine way of knowing. Feminine knowing comes through receptivity, not assertion; through intuition, not analysis; through the feeling intellect, not the intellect of cold reason. The communion between mother and child is a kind of knowing that comes through loving: it is a kind of visionary awareness.

This is not to say that women are always right and men always wrong; or that women are more often right than wrong. That is to argue at a trivial level. I am pleading for us all to think more seriously and more deeply of what a human person really is; and of what a really mature human person really is. Just as the Christians outthought and outlived other ideas about human persons and human relationships in the ancient world in the light of Christ's person and Christ's teaching, may it not be among our primary duties in this modern predicament of humanity that we should re-think and re-express that primal affirmation: 'So God created man in his own image: in the image of God he created him: male and female he created them.' Unless we think more seriously and more deeply about gender, about maleness and femaleness, about the inner attitude of each of us and about the way we understand and respect and dance with each other, then our Western civilisation will be hastened all the more rapidly to its self-destruction.

You will have heard it said, possibly you may have said it yourself when face to face with some tragic happening. Why does God allow such a thing as this to happen? Why doesn't God prevent it?

If you reflect on what you have said and ask what assumptions about the character of God lie behind it, you will see that your question implies a particular idea of the kind of God your God is. Your question implies that God, in your view of him, is some kind of all-powerful potentate, an unpredictable, capricious manipulator of the universe, able to control everything that happens as if he were the operator of a complex electronic switchboard of a computerised universal network.

But if God were like that, all-powerful, able and ready to do anything and everything, what would it be like to be a human being in a world manipulated by such a ruler? Where would be our freedom? Where would be our humanity? At best we would be slaves, robots, daleks. There can be no freedom without risk, no humanity without pain.

The Christmas stories, if we reflect on them, propose a very different idea of the kind of God the God of Christmas is. The God to whom the Christmas stories point is not at all an all-powerful manipulator of history, but one who puts himself at risk in the historical enterprise of which we believe him to be the author. The strength of the Christian God is the strength of weakness.

The birth of any child is a marvellous happening, biologically and humanly marvellous. As each child grows up, things will sometimes, as we say, 'come right', sometimes 'come wrong'. Whenever a husband and wife decide to give birth to a new being, to give birth to a child, they are setting in motion a process they can never wholly control, and indeed beyond a certain age must not try to control. To give life to another is to release into the stream of human existence a new animated centre of choices and actions, full of possibilities of both good and harm.

We who are parents do just this: we take a tremendous risk from a motive of creative love. What results from our act of love may turn out to be very different from what we had hoped. What parent is there who has not been made to suffer the sight of the loved child making choices likely to cause damage to others as well as to himself. We know what it is to be powerless. Our power to give life to a new being is counterbalanced by our powerlessness to control what happens as our child grows into adult independence. Certainly we are powerless to shield our child from the accidents of life. In spite of all the accidents and the distresses, however, I doubt if there are many parents who, looking back on the joys and the pains of family life, would say that they wished they had never given birth to their children.

If we find it worth the risk to give birth to new beings in all their freedom and vulnerability, perhaps we can begin to understand the risk that God takes in enabling such beings as we are with all our capacity for love and for destruction; and to say that even this risk of human history is something we would not wish to have been otherwise. The price of freedom is Love's experience of powerlessness to interfere to avert disaster.

The child of Bethlehem was scourged, crowned with thorns, mocked, and nailed to a gibbet, and the Love that gave him being was powerless to interfere. Only Jesus could have prevented the cross had he been willing to compromise and to deny the truth that claimed him. For God to intervene and to prevent this outcome would have been to deny his very truth, his very love. Mary at the cross is the symbol of every parent who has experienced the death in youth or early manhood of the child she carried in her womb with so much hope. In our east window Mary stands at the cross and is unable to do anything to save her son. All she can do is to go on loving through her grief and tears.

The Christmas stories then are telling us not so much about Jesus as about God. God, they are saying, is to be thought of as one who like a parent exposes himself to all the pain and suffering that may be hidden in the act of giving birth to a new being who has freedom to choose. The cross is the shape that divine love takes in such a world as ours. But just as a parent goes on loving through the pain, so the Christmas stories point us to God as one whose love is unfailing, indestructible. The worst that evil can do to such a love is to give this love ever fresh opportunities of loving. Our hope lies in the indestructibility of God's love. His love will find a way, even if the way to life is through death. The cross which in the east window is a gallows to which the dead Jesus is nailed becomes in the new cross on the High Altar a radiance of glory. The bronze figure of the Walking Madonna in the Close, striding into the world's distress with purposeful compassion, is a symbol of suffering transfigured, a symbol of the Christian community of the resurrection animated with the energy of new life, of caring love.

These Christmas stories then are far more than bedtime tales for toddlers. They are really for adults only as they wrestle with the complexities and contradictions of being divine and being human. They illuminate that intermingling of joy and woe that make up our adult experience. As William Blake memorably put it:

> Man is made for joy and woe,
> And when this we rightly know,
> Thro' the world we safely go.

We can only celebrate Christmas and enter into its joy and hope, if we will also open our imagination and our heart to the sufferings of others. To experience the pain of our own helplessness will take us nearer to the heart of God in whose powerlessness lies his great strength and our sure hope.

Here we meet the central paradox of the manger and the cross. God's power is revealed in his powerlessness. His power is the power of a love which cannot coerce or compel but can only call forth from us a love-response. And woven into the long history of the human race is the shining evidence of Love the artist making beauty out of the unpromising raw materials of our temperament and our circumstances. As William Blake again so clearly saw:

> Joy and woe are woven fine,
> A clothing for the soul divine.

The globe and the map are two ways of providing us with a vital model of planet earth. There's the globe model, the earth in the round spinning on its axis; and there is that flat model on the first pages of the school atlas – Mercator's Projection – as if the world were an orange and the skin had been peeled off and laid out flat. It is an excellent teaching aid but nothing like the cosmos. That is how St Luke tells the story of Jesus. St John, however, presents the story more as a kind of globe, a story in the round in which elements are interrelated. Interpretation is woven into recollection; history and mystery flow into and out of each other. Luke's story of the going up to heaven of Jesus forty days after his resurrection was for the poet Stevie Smith what she called one of those 'beautifully painted fairy stories pretending to be true'. There is no story in John as of an event, an observed ascension, but rather a sense throughout the Gospel that this one of whose life all these things are being said is the crucified one who is alive beyond death, the human one now passed out of time and history but present within history and time as animating presence after a quite different manner and mode.

If Ascension Day were to be renamed the Feast of the Ascended Christ, then much of the problem element would be removed. The emphasis would be on an abiding truth rather than on an event which, if taken literally as one in a sequence of events, obstructs the truth it is intended to express. Heaven is a word-symbol for that dimension of reality we indicate when we speak of God.

What I believe we celebrate on Ascension Day is the Feast of the Glorious Availability of Christ. The Christ of our faith abides for ever and is accessible for ever as our indestructible point of reference beyond history, the source from beyond ourselves of the 'courage to be' in the ambiguities and trials of our own circumstances. This is the real emphasis of the New Testament writers and of the faith of the Christian communities of the centuries.

It is not an event then, observed and recorded, that holds the centre of our faith. What holds the centre of our faith is the present ascendancy of our Lord. This Jesus, this life that ended in ignominious disgrace and death, is the life which has been vindicated and lifted high; and the evidence is the continuing power of this life once lived on earth to affect men and women all these centuries later opening up within us now new attitudes, new energies, new powers of loving.

By keeping Ascension Day we not only affirm the glorious availability of Christ, we also affirm the essential if mysterious connection between the Christ of our faith now and the Jesus who was at the centre of those events nearly 2,000 years ago. The simple story told by Luke of the disciples seeing the risen Jesus being received up into the cloud was one way of making this connection between the Jesus of history and the Christ of faith. And what could have been more natural for a writer of the first century, for whom the earth was flat and heaven the abode of God, conceived of as above the flat earth? The more philosophical author of the Fourth Gospel makes the same connection in a different way. He presents Jesus as saying to his disciples before his death: 'I came forth from the Father and am come into the world; again I leave the world and go to the Father.' This is the same belief differently presented, the same truth presented in a different metaphor.

Let us not dismiss Luke, however, as a naïve narrator. He too is a symbolic theologian. Even this seemingly simple story of the ascension of Jesus is, when you really examine it, as symbolic in character as Luke's story of Pentecost with the tongues of fire and the rushing mighty wind. The cloud into which Jesus is said to be received is a metaphor with a long Old Testament usage as a symbol for the Presence of God, veiling the glory that it represents. When you really examine Luke's whole method of presenting the things concerning Jesus you find that he is a theologian using the story form to interpret the mystery that is present in the history.

If we were to abandon the celebration of our Lord's Ascension on the grounds that this image confuses those who do not understand the way the biblical writers use metaphor and symbol, we would not only impoverish our Christian year but diminish our Christian vision. For this effulgence of glory belongs to the very heart of our Christian understanding of the relationship between man and God. What else ultimately saves human experience from dust and ashes except our vision of Christ as the glory of God in the life of a man? For in the words of St Irenaeus, 'The glory of God is a man fully alive; the life of a man is the vision of God.'

All Saints-tide in any year bursts through the November gloom like a blazing shaft of sunlight. Once again our hearts dance to the words and the music of the All Saints-tide hymns of which for me Peter Abelard's twelfth-century vision of a heavenly Jerusalem is supreme:

> Wish and fulfilment can severed be ne'er,
> Nor the thing prayed for come short of the prayer.

'Wishful thinking', sneers the cynic. ' "Vision of peace" that brings joy evermore!' reply the saints of all the ages, and not least of our own.

A Christian lives life with two calendars. There is the calendar of the seasons, the calendar in which time is divided up into months and weeks and days, studded with sorrows and with joys, and with long usual times. And there is for the Christian another calendar of times and seasons which lifts him out of time and into eternity. For eternity has broken into time; eternity is here, is now. The Christian calendar is made up of the great events in the remembered and symbolised life of Jesus as those events have become treasured and celebrated down the centuries within the community of faith. Christmas, Easter, Pentecost. These first; but then, with the years, other events in the remembered life of Jesus have been given their symbolic place in the Christian calendar. Added to the events concerning Jesus are the events concerning his mother, his first disciples, and all subsequent disciples and confessors and martyrs – a galaxy of glorious names of well-graced men and women whose Christian virtues have been recognised, recorded and canonised. The pages of human history are illuminated with the names of Polycarp and Augustine, Francis and the Lady Julian, Teresa of Avila and Charles de Foucauld. And far outnumbering the known saints are the saints unknown by name to the Church but well known to God.

The saints are real; they have been and they are; and nothing can remove from the pages of human history the record of their faithfulness to the vision that beckoned them and the love they lavished on all who came within the radiance of their love.

I never cease to be moved by the story of the death of the French parish-priest, the Abbé Huvelin, who was a source of spiritual help to hundreds of his contemporaries. Lifting himself from his camp-bed in the vestry of his church in Paris – where he had insisted on being during his last illness so that he could be available to those who needed him – he stretched out his arms towards a crucifix on the wall opposite and said: 'I can never love enough'. So died a man whose whole life had been given to God to be a channel of God's love to others.

Baron von Hügel used to speak of the need for what he called 'homely heroism', heroism nearer home. Our temptation is to see circumstances as frustration rather than opportunity. In fact our circumstances are the raw material of our growth as persons towards ever more enriching humanness and holiness. If you study the lives of the saints, whether the well-known saints about whom much is known and written or those little-known saints, the 'blessed Chiones' who keep love in circulation, ask yourself what they have in common. You will find that one thing they have in common is that they have accepted the harsh circumstances of life as the raw materials of holiness; they obey the command of Christ to take up the cross of their harsh circumstances and follow him. Sanctity is the alternative to cynicism, homely heroism the alternative to resentment, bitterness, self-pity, and defeat.

The saints declare by what they are that what has happened can happen again. Human nature has been changed and can be changed. It requires grace to turn a man into a saint and he who denies it does not know what either a man or a saint is. All Saints' Day is the evidence of the reality of grace, of God's enabling help, and an invitation to us all to seek again this grace of our Lord Jesus Christ. What above all is asked of us is that we shall not be disobedient to the heavenly vision. What is asked of us is that we shall in the end be found to have done the best things in the worst times and to have hoped them in the most calamitous.

What else can the weeks of Lent be about if not about growth – growth in penitence and prayer; growth in our knowledge of God and of ourselves; of ourselves in relation to God; of God in relation to ourselves; of Christ as God's chief word to us and of our responsive word of faith to God.

There are many opportunities for growth in prayer; and by prayer I mean a spiritual relationship, of openness as between two friends; a kind of breathing, an interior attitude and desire which permeates our days as our breathing permeates our days without our noticing it. But, as the Russian pilgrim discovered, the ceaseless prayer of the heart like the ceaseless movement of the lungs is a consequence of other things being in a good healthy condition. So in Lent we shall do well to examine the condition of our praying, and that includes examining the condition of our penitence.

Penitence speaks of a kind of honesty – about being honest to God about ourselves. I know nothing more difficult than trying to be honest to God about myself. It is not that I am afraid of being honest to God; it is just so difficult to know if I am really being honest about myself. It is not that I am afraid of facing the truth about myself; it is just so difficult to be sure what the truth is.

Wanting to be honest to God about ourselves is therefore a necessary part of prayer; wanting to be free of all self-deception, all evasiveness, all deviousness; of all self-pity, all fear, all pretence; wanting to recover that single-mindedness of which our Lord was speaking when he said: 'Blest are those who are pure in heart for they shall see God'. This purity of heart can only mean the singleness of mind and of desire which comes when we allow the Holy Spirit to simplify our lives at the centre. This I believe is the essence of holiness, the glorious secret which our Lord invites us to explore and discover.

All true spiritual growth is towards simplicity of heart and singleness of desire, so that whatever comes to us of pain or hurt, of bereavement or failure, of sin or harm done to others, can be burnt up in the crucible of Christ's loving presence in our heart and become in us a purged and purified love for others.

'Take my yoke upon you and learn from me: for I am gentle and lowly of heart; and you will find rest for your souls.'

The Apostle Paul continues to get an undeservedly bad press from those who have never tried to enter into his life and thought. Some dismiss him as a chauvinistic anti-feminist and forget that it was from his mind and heart and hand that we received the sublime poem about love in I Corinthians 13. Others dismiss him as a thinker too tortuous and rabbinic to be bothered with, and forget how influential again and again in the course of the Christian centuries has been his letter to the Romans, his teaching about justification by faith in contrast to the Pharisaic straitjacket of obedience to the letter of the law. It was another Paul, Paul Tillich, who brilliantly encapsulated the heart of this teaching – 'learning to accept that we are accepted by God in spite of knowing ourselves to be unacceptable'.

Whatever we think or feel about the Apostle Paul, there is no denying that the swift spread of the good news of God's reconciling presence in Jesus Christ was in large part due to his faith and courage. Our Christianity would have been an immeasurably poorer thing and our world an immeasurably poorer place had not this particular man met with an experience on the Damascus road that changed his whole attitude and way of life. He did that most difficult of all things – he acknowledged that all his life up to that point had been lived on false assumptions and wrong expectations.

There is one sentence connected with Paul's conversion and subsequent persecution and imprisonment which never leaves me alone. It occurs in Paul's defence before King Agrippa as given by Luke in the book of Acts. After speaking of his former life and his subsequent life, Paul says: 'Wherefore, O King Agrippa, I was not disobedient to the heavenly vision'. When you remember all that Paul actually suffered in the course of his pilgrimages as a messenger of Christ these words strike the reader as the understatement of all time. Was ever the command of Jesus, 'Follow me', so obeyed?

What haunts me is the double negative: 'I was not disobedient . . . ' When I ask of my own discipleship, can I truthfully claim that I have been 'not disobedient' to the heavenly vision?

The only reason why anyone is a Christian is that he or she knows themselves claimed by a vision. We know, having once felt the claim, that we could not be disobedient to that vision without denying a truth that is so woven into the fabric of our most intimate self that the denial would be a betrayal of oneself as well as a betrayal of Christ.

Having acknowledged that claim of Christ many years ago, I believe I can almost just say of my desire, of my intention, of the innermost direction of my will, 'I have been not disobedient to the heavenly vision'. However, it is when I ask myself of the actual quality of my being 'not disobedient' that I become saddened into penitence. For when you move from the double negative to the positive and ask about the quality and faithfulness of your actual obedience, the feebleness and the failures are declared – not so much deliberate failures of intention but actual feebleness of following.

Christ by giving us a vision of God in his teaching and his whole manner of life lays claim on our allegiance to that vision once we have seen it. What we find difficult is deciding just what this allegiance requires of us in terms of the way we live. How are we so to live that the heavenly vision colours the whole style and manner of our living?

Someone said that the hallmark of intelligence is to see the point and make the necessary connections. I believe it is more than the hallmark of intelligence: I believe it is also the hallmark of moral seriousness. There is a necessary connection between seeing the truth and doing the truth. Once we have seen it we must set about doing it; otherwise we betray the truth we acknowledge to be true. Paul saw that truth on the Damascus road and made the necessary connections for the rest of his life to the point of martyrdom. He was not disobedient to the heavenly vision.

One of the advantages of modern translations of the Bible done by scholars is that sometimes they not only clarify the meaning of the text, but do so with a turn of phrase that opens up a new line of thought. Those who decided what should be the readings for the Sunday Eucharist in the Alternative Service Book chose the translation of each selected passage which in their judgement best brought out the meaning of the passage selected. As literature these modern translations may not have the resonance of the Authorised Version. But as communications of meaning they are frequently superior.

This is true especially of some of the more obscure passages in the Letters of the Apostle Paul. There is a passage in his Letter to the Romans where the translation of the Jerusalem Bible is especially vivid. Paul is drawing the contrast between attitudes he calls 'spiritual' and attitudes he calls 'unspiritual'. This translation reads: 'It is death to limit oneself to what is unspiritual'. It is the phrase 'to limit oneself' which I find most illuminating. For this is exactly what vast numbers of human beings are doing. This way of putting the matter goes to the very root of our present human predicament. It correctly expresses what is happening within our Western culture.

In 1932 Archbishop William Temple entitled the third of his Gifford Lectures *Nature, Man and God*, with the subtitle 'The Cartesian Faux-Pas'. He was writing about the false step in thinking which emanated from the mind of the philosopher Descartes and has become the unchallenged assumption on the basis of which most of our Western way of life has been developed in the last three hundred years. What Descartes did was to separate in thought what in reality belong together. He divided body from mind and set going a whole process which separated the material from the human. Modern medicine, for example, takes the form it does largely because it is based on a limited view of the nature of a human person, treating the body as a kind of mechanism and failing to understand what a human person is in his or her wholeness and complexity. Modern medicine for the most part has limited itself to a view of human beings for which Paul's word is 'unspiritual'. This view of the human body as an organism capable of being treated as a kind of biological machine is a way of thinking which derives not only from the thinking of Descartes, but also from the thinking of Newton who interprets the whole universe as a kind of machine.

By allowing this bent assumption to get into our Western way of thinking for 300 years, by allowing this mechanistic way of thinking to become the assumption on which we habitually act, we in the West have developed our sciences and our technologies. Without question great material benefits have resulted from this Cartesian-Newtonian way of looking at our world and discovering how to manipulate the energies of nature. One need not detail the advantages for social life of the achievements of science and technology. But what is becoming increasingly clear to those people who are not imprisoned within the Cartesian dogma is that the predicament we are in does in large part come from a false way of thinking about the true nature of things and the true nature of persons. 'It is death', says St Paul, 'to limit oneself to what is unspiritual.' What is mechanistic is unspiritual. To treat human beings and human societies as if they were machines is to invite disaster. 'Social engineering', 'genetic engineering', are tell-tale expressions, clearly indicating a mechanistic state of mind.

Not all is yet lost. It was the historian Arnold Toynbee who in his study of the rise and fall of civilisations declared that every civilisation nourished within itself the seeds of its own decay. There have been many efforts at civilisation over the centuries: many great experiments and achievements are now mere ruins with a few remaining artefacts on display in museums. Yet within a disintegrating civilisation there are also the seeds of new birth, of creative change. Under the threat of disintegration we are beginning to clarify our minds about the falsehood which we have for so long taken to be the truth. Unexpectedly a great doubt about accepted scientific theory on the nature of the material universe has come from scientists themselves who are working in the area of sub-atomic particles. These high priests of new science are no longer as sure about what they thought they knew as were their predecessors. The more they probe into the way things are, the more complex and puzzling is what they are finding. Things no longer fit so neatly into the previously constructed compartments of knowledge. This new thinking sees the universe as systems of interrelated energies; it is breaking down the artificial walls between different branches of science, demanding a revision of basic assumptions and former certainties. This new perception that everything is related to other things and not to be treated in isolation is arising partly from the investigations of scientists and partly from popular protests about the destructive effects on the environment of what we have for far too long been so blindly doing.

In the science of ecology – the scientific investigation of the interrelatedness of all living organisms – lies hope. Ecology is not spirituality, but it is a different way of looking at our world and at our human behaviour in our world, which does not allow us any longer to use the mechanistic model. By destroying the false thinking based on the idea that everything can be treated as a kind of machine, it opens our minds to the recovery of a truer perception of the nature of human persons, of human need and of human society.

Once we begin to admit the interrelatedness of body and mind, of man and nature, of social behaviour and natural resources, the interrelatedness of the physical and the emotional, the intellectual and the imaginative, then we are challenging the basic assumptions of the scientists, of current economies and therefore of business enterprise, of government policies, of industrial processes. We open doors of perception on to the whole vast question of what is truly valuable. What are the values that really matter? The more we do this in the way we think, the more we shall be opening our minds again in our secular age to the recognition that there is more in life than can be identified by the exercise of the rational intellect. We can again open our minds to recognise that other dimension of reality to which as Christians we point when we speak the word 'God' – the claim upon us of this mysterious Other of whom Paul speaks in this passage from his Letter to the Christians at Rome: 'Life and peace come only with concern for the spiritual. That is because to limit oneself to what is unspiritual is to be at enmity with God.'

To be at odds with God is to be at odds with true human well-being. To be at odds with God is to misuse the world of nature and misapply the given resources of energy. Ecology is not spirituality; but it is nearer to true thinking about what is real and what is unreal and what makes for human well-being. Getting our thinking right about the nature of things is a necessity for individuals and for nations. For Christians correct thinking is a special obligation. We are commanded to love God with all our mind as well as with all our heart.

The prologue to St John's Gospel is a kind of theological poem using powerful images – word, light and darkness, birth, glory. 'In the beginning was the Word, and the Word was with God and the Word was God.' Contrast that with the kind of statement that might be made by an astrophysical scientist. 'In the beginning was the hot, big bang.'

The majority of physicists nowadays seem to be saying that the origin of the universe was a mighty explosion; and when they speak of the universe as expanding they are saying that the material objects that came into existence as a result of the excessive heat generated by the explosion are rushing away from each other into space at a great speed. But when St John says 'In the beginning was the Word,' and when the modern scientist says 'In the beginning was the hot, big bang,' they are not contradicting each other: they are not talking about the same things at all.

The scientist is speaking about origins; the evangelist is speaking about meanings. The scientist is speaking about the what, the when, and the how; the evangelist is speaking about the why and the whither. The science story of how the universe began in no way cancels out the evangelist's story about what it means. The science story that has been developed over the last 200 years about the origin of the material universe is a theory based on observation, calculation and speculation. It is a fascinating theory: no wonder it captures the imagination of intelligent young people and is thought by many of them to have put an end to all talk about God. And when we add to the fascination of the story that scientists tell about origins and evolutions, and the amazing success of science-based technology, it is not at all surprising if the young regard the stories of the Bible – and especially the story of the creation of the world in the book of Genesis – as so much 'old hat', man's early gropings after knowledge and explanation now to be discarded in the bright light of scientific information.

When St John says 'In the beginning was the Word,' he is not talking about an event like a big bang. He is not talking about origins at all; he is not talking about the first event in a time-sequence of events. He is talking about that which exists beyond time – about another dimension of reality altogether.

There is one question about origins that you can put to a scientist for which he has no answer: 'Why is there something and not nothing?' His science does not enable him to give an answer. His science only begins when there is something tangible that can be measured. Christian belief claims that before the world was, God is. He is the author. And when the evangelist in this prologue talks about creation he is really talking about revelation, about the unveiling of what is, about disclosure. John's choice of the symbol 'the Word' makes it clear that he is talking about communication. His use of the image of light speaks of making sight possible. The light shines in the darkness and is a light of such power that the darkness cannot overmaster it. This is the light that enlightens every man and enables him to see, not merely with physical eyes but with understanding.

The scientific way of exploring the physical universe is not the way to all knowledge. Science opens the doors to a vast but limited range of knowledge; and if you speak with a top scientist he will be the first to explain the limitations of scientific method and knowledge. How else could so many top scientists be also men of religious faith if they were not clear in their minds that science has not taken the place of religion, but rather that science itself exists within a larger mystery of meaning? The larger mystery is ourselves: self-conscious human beings trying to live in communities with other self-conscious human beings and asking fundamental questions reaching to the very boundaries of experience. Who am I? What may I hope? What should I do? A human being is not just a complex biological organism , he is an 'animal that hopes'. His curiosity lies at the base both of his science and of his religion. He is not content with knowing what; his deeper question is why. He is not content, as other animals are, with a small range of instinctive needs and reactions. Man is a problem to himself. Man the scientist in his explorations of the galaxies and the atoms shows himself to be a restless creature who seeks for light in his darkness, but often gets stuck within the narrow confines of the methods of science. Man cannot live by science alone. The world of art, music, literature, religion is the evidence that human beings do not live by science alone. Too much of the teaching of science in schools and universities has failed to set science within this larger context of mystery and meaning. Complex questions of the relation of science and its truths to politics, economics, morals, art, philosophy and religion have been blithely ignored. Many scientists and teachers of science who dismiss the claims of religion are themselves quite unaware of modern methods of interpreting religious traditions and beliefs. Many teachers of religious subjects in schools are equally ignorant of the truths and the limitations of science. Both sets of teachers are often ill-equipped to deal with the tricky interface of religious and scientific approaches to the origins of the universe and the meaning and mystery of human experience. There are some Christians who refuse to work out the relation between science and religion; and there are some scientists who believe that there is no need to work out the relation between science and religion. Religion for them is no more than a relic of a past age.

Wearing blinkers may be necessary for carthorses; it is disastrous for human beings in a world such as ours. Many Christians are retreating from reality, from the real life of the real world, into a closed thought-world based on a view of the character and authority of the writings of the Bible which I, for one, do not believe to be a correct view of the true meaning and significance of those writings.

Reflect once more on the central affirmation of the Gospel when John says that this revealing 'Word' which was in the beginning with God, which indeed was God, was made flesh and dwelt among us. This word that God speaks to the human race *is* Jesus. God speaks to the human race in a form and in a language which all humans can understand and to which all humans can respond – in the person of a man: a man like all of us and yet a man who speaks to us as no other person speaks. But what God is saying to us in this Word embodied in a human historical life is not a Word that human beings find it easy to accept. The Prologue says: 'He was in the world and the world was made through him, yet the world knew him not. He came to his own home and his own people received him not.'

The enfleshed Word of God embodied in the man Jesus was crucified by a conspiracy of frightened men holding positions of power in the Church-state of Israel in a country occupied by the military forces of imperial Rome. But there were some who heard and received this Word which became flesh and dwelt among them 'full of grace and truth'. There were some who saw in and through the human a glory, 'the glory as of the only Son from the Father'. You and I are in that company of those who see and believe; who partly see and partly believe. It is our desire to help others to see what we see. Such is the general state of mind of our Western world that the assumptions on which more and more of our contemporaries live and move and choose and decide are assumptions based on a false view of what constitutes knowledge. They cannot see the glory of God in the face of Jesus Christ; they cannot believe that there is a Word that is addressed to them in all that Jesus said and did, which opens up for them a whole new dimension of self-understanding, of what is real, of what really matters. They cannot see the grace, the truth and the glory because they have become imprisoned in a narrow view of the way things are. What we have to get rid of from our schools and colleges, from the programmes on television and radio, from newspapers and magazines, is bad science and bad theology.

By far the biggest task the Church has to undertake is an intellectual task, in no way less demanding than the intellectual task of the first four centuries. It is the task of disabusing human minds of false assumptions about the truth of the way things are – as a prelude to re-education in the mystery and the meaning of being alive and being human. For the continuing creative work of the Word of God made flesh and dwelling among us is to make and keep the human race truly human. Human beings can only become all that they have it in them to become if they will respond in faith and prayer and desire to the Word of God which is dwelling among us and claiming us from darkness and destruction into his own glorious light.

The most intoxicating word in any language is the word 'freedom'. Shouted from the barricades in any revolution in any nationality it can arouse men's passions and drive men to deeds of desperate daring – though too often men find too late that the removal of one oppressor only opens the door for another. Freedom is a word of many facets: it swings between the personal and the political. Both extremes are expressed in the literature of the Bible. In the experiences of Israel, captivity and liberation alternate with the ebb and flow of power and weakness. Captives in Egypt, set free for a new homeland after long journeys through the wilderness. Captives in Babylon, set free for return and reconstruction of Jerusalem. Captivity interpreted as the consequence of disobedience to the will of Yahweh. Restoration interpreted as the sign of Yahweh's merciful forgiveness and faithfulness to his side of the covenant which he had made with the ancestors – Abraham, Isaac and Jacob.

The political polarities of the Old Testament sagas become the personal polarities of the teaching of Jesus and the teaching of Paul. The idea of political captivity is transferred to become a way of speaking about interior personal captivity. Healing in the ministry of Jesus is often spoken of as a setting free from captivity. There is a vivid account in Luke of the healing by Jesus of a 'woman who had had a spirit of infirmity for eighteen years: she was bent over and could not fully straighten herself'? Jesus laid his hands on her and she was made straight. When challenged by the ruler of the synagogue for doing an act of healing on the Sabbath day Jesus replied: 'Ought not this woman, a daughter of Abraham whom Satan bound for eighteen years, to be loosed from her bond on the Sabbath day?'

Certain kinds of physical infirmity are understood by medical people today to be the consequence of some inner unresolved emotional problems. Jesus spoke of these inner emotional disorders as bonds preventing people from being free – free to be open, free to be self-giving. He spoke of being in captivity to sin, to some unresolved guilt. He spoke of being in captivity to fear; and, as we all know, fear of this or that can have a serious inhibiting effect in a person's life. So we find growing up within the Christian communities of the early centuries this conviction that to believe in the presence and power of Christ is to be in touch with an energy which can liberate people into a freer, fuller, happier life.

'I am come', says Jesus in St John, 'that you may have life and have it in all its fullness.' And Paul in one of his visionary passages coins that exhilarating expression: 'The creation itself will be set free from its bondage to decay and obtain the *glorious liberty* of the children of God'. Do we enjoy our Christianity as a glorious liberty – a liberty given by God to those who know themselves to be his sons and are eager to live in our time and in our world as sons of God should live? What is the way into this promised freedom? Again in St John Jesus says: 'If you continue in my word, you are truly my disciples and you will know the truth, and the truth will make you free.'

The way into this promised freedom is indeed a way – to walk in, to continue in. We are to live as those who continue in Christ's word. The way is the way of discipleship. We shall come to know the truth if we follow in the way of discipleship, and the more we come to know the truth and to do the truth, the more we shall enter into the glorious liberty of the sons of God. For truth in St John's use of it is not an intellectual knowing like philosophy or mathematics. Truth in St John's use of it is a way of living which leads the disciple into a kind of knowing which is the knowing of a person of Christ as the uniquely Spirit-filled person – a knowing which is also an obeying. And what are we to obey? We are to obey Christ's command which is to love with the kind of love with which we ourselves are loved by God.

The way into freedom is a way of relationship which means allowing ourselves to be open to hear and receive the word. This word is both the words that Jesus spoke and the word that Jesus is. For Jesus is for us the word of God: he is in all that he is and does what God is saying to us and what God wants us to respond to, so that we may know the truth, which is both the truth about ourselves and the truth about Christ, and therefore the way for us into freedom – the 'glorious liberty' of the children of God.

What is this freedom? It is freedom from all that holds us in captivity, all that harms our life and prevents our growth; freedom from sin and feelings of guilt, freedom from fear in all its myriad forms, freedom from self-rejection and self-pity, freedom from small-mindedness and self-enclosure; freedom from all that and therefore freedom for growth into those qualities and dispositions which are the dispositions of Christ and the fruit of his Spirit; freedom to give ourselves to the depth of our being to the Divine Charity, to God himself, the ultimate Reality.

Do you believe this? Deep down in your hearts do you really believe that God is and that God is loving us out of what we are towards that better person that each of us is capable of becoming? Do you really believe that your life is a gift to be developed, the raw material of something to be made glorious if we will cooperate with God in the making of ourselves what in his eyes we already are? Do you allow yourselves to believe that you are important, that you matter, that you have value? Do we ever deeply consider within ourselves that the real value of our lives is the value we have to God and the value other people find in us? And do we see what this implies? It implies that our essential task is to cooperate with God with strong desire and continuing prayer.

Faith, desire and prayer: by this threefold yet single route we shall be guided if we trust the Spirit into all the truth, the truth that will make us free from all self-seeking, all self-rejection, all false self-importance; free for a life of self-giving, free to love God, free to love our neighbour, free to love ourselves as we come to rejoice in the strangest truth of all, that we – you and I – are surprisingly loved by God.

If you were asked to make a list of what you value most, I wonder if your list would include the experience of friendship. I should place friendship very high on my list of what I value most; and there is something very special about the friendships one makes in the privileged years of college and university life. For me certainly it is the friends I made as a student rather than the friends I made as a schoolboy who have continued with me in all the years since. There were so many shared experiences in the exploration of a world as yet only partly known but already opening up.

It is not that one sees much of these friends in subsequent years – each goes his different way. But you have only to meet for an hour or a day and you find yourself as it were taking up the relationship where you last left it, as if it had been continuing underground for all the years in between. The heart and centre of this kind of friendship is the sense of knowing and being known, of accepting and of being accepted. To know yourself to be known and accepted is one of life's best gifts.

In the exchanges between friends meeting again after long absence there is no inquisitive curiosity. What is said by each is what each chooses to say. What is offered is what is accepted in a mutual exchange. True friendship is wonderfully free of possessiveness or of censoriousness. Each respects the other's privacy and freedom; each receives whatever the other chooses to disclose of pain or predicament. Friendship consists in giving and taking whatever there is to give and take. There is no trace of pretence, no need for cover-up, no place for jealousy or defensiveness, no desire to impress. It is a very special gift at the receiving end of friendship to be known and to know that one is known for what one is, to be accepted and to know that one is accepted for what one is. But there would be no such gift if this experience were not reciprocal, given as well as received.

I believe we each of us needs to be known. As children certainly we each need to know ourselves known by our parents and accepted for what we are. This being known and accepted gives us basic confidence for knowing and accepting ourselves. Not to know oneself known and accepted leaves a legacy of self-doubt, uncertainty, even self-rejection. But as adults also we each need to know ourselves known and accepted for what we are. Surely this is what genuinely Christian community relationships are meant to be. When Jesus says to his disciples 'You are my friends', he goes on to say 'I want you to love one another as I love you'. And what is this love of which he speaks if not a relationship of being known and of being accepted?

There is a significant difference, however, between the chance friendships of our youth and the chosen friendships of the Christian community. The chance friendships result from whatever it is that attracts us to each other, whatever it is that enables us to trust one another and just enjoy being together, doing things together. Chance friendships grow out of feelings of affinity, out of discovery of shared interest; but if they are to last through life they need to be kept in repair.

In the Christian community we do not so much respond in friendship on the basis of attraction and affinity, we respond because we have been chosen and given to each other. Within the community of the baptised we grow up to understand the marvellous truth of the words of Jesus, 'You are my friends'. St John in his Gospel presentation of Jesus and of the significance of Jesus makes our relationships with each other in the Christian community depend on his relationship with us; and the significance of this in St John's presentation lies in the relationship of Jesus to the one greater than he whom he addresses as Father. At its deepest level what is being said is that the universe into which we are born without any choice on our part is not a hostile or threatening unknown. At the heart of the universe is a divine benevolence, an ultimate love to be responded to as you would respond to a loving father. And what is being further said by this Jesus – whose relationship to this loving Father is presented by St John in his Gospel as the central truth – is that he draws us to himself and gives us to each other so that a love of brethren shall prevail over all other attitudes. We shall be friends within a society of friends whose friendship with each other draws its strength from a greater friendship which is God's friendship for each of us. As Christian men and women we are required over and above the natural to cultivate and keep in good repair those chosen friendships based on the command of Jesus that we shall love one another as he loves us. Christian friendship is an expression of self-forgetful concentration on the true well-being of the other.

When I was very young, there were two words that I heard frequently from the lips of my parents, my grandparents, my aunts and uncles – the words 'right' and 'wrong'. I grew up with a strong sense that actions belonged to one or other of these categories. What people did, what I did, fell into one category or the other. And they all seemed very clear in their own minds which were the actions that came under the label 'wrong'.

I say this not in any way to criticise – still less to mock – these good people. I say it rather to indicate the great differences between then and now. These elders and betters of my youth were not exceptional. Generally speaking, in working-class and middle-class families of the 1920s there was agreement about what kind of behaviour was to be called right, what kind of behaviour was to be called wrong. Divorce was wrong; birth control was wrong; buying things by hire purchase before you had saved up the necessary money was wrong; not speaking the truth was very definitely wrong.

Social disapproval and even legal penalties were able to control public and private morality within agreed limits. Today in Western society not only is this not so as a matter of fact, but there is also no consensus of what is morally right or wrong. You can observe a similar change in attitudes to what is acceptable and what is not acceptable in the world of sport. What then has happened to break down this previously held general consensus of what kind of behaviour was acceptable and what not? What are the acids that have eaten into this previously strong structure of safeguards of social morality? It is not difficult to make a list: the First World War and the frightfulness of what civilised nations did to each other; the economic collapse of the late '20s and very early '30s, and consequent unemployment; the Second World War and the breaking up of neighbourhoods and families; the postwar growth of the mass media – radio and later television bringing into people's homes evidence of quite different ideas of morality which led people to question the validity of the patterns and assumptions of previous decades. All this and much else weakened the stance of the traditional social moral structures until the consensus building collapsed and we found ourselves in a new kind of society which we learned to call 'pluralist' – meaning that there were many options not one agreed morality. More and more did novels and plays and actual behaviour call in question the validity of the old moral codes and rules and disapprovals. We heard the phrase 'situation ethics'. There were no longer clear rules to be obeyed; each person must reach his or her own decisions about what to do in particular situations. Everything was relative, nothing was absolute.

This shattering of the moral foundations and structures of previous generations was not, however, wholly destructive. A new sense of the value of persons developed, a great deal of hypocrisy was eliminated. The absence of rules and social sanctions meant that individuals had to work out for themselves what would be their attitude and their action. In all this there was a kind of growing out of dependence on rules and the fear of what people would think into a more mature and responsible attitude to the making of moral decisions.

Of course there have been casualties in a period of upheaval and uncertainty. The increase in divorces has radically affected families. There has been a devaluation of honesty and a growing disregard for truth. And I cannot believe that the loss of the ideal of service as the principle that should govern behaviour is not itself a casualty.

In and through all this has been a withdrawal of large numbers of people from public worship, a discarding of the Christian teaching about man's place in the universe, an ignorance of the dimension of transcendence, of the authority and claims of God. Disbelief is more widespread than belief. Selfishness and greed are rampant. Yet there is also evidence of a strong sense of the need for serious thinking about the human predicament and about new developments that are taking place as a result of the changes brought about by science and technology.

In our Anglican tradition we have always affirmed the importance of reason, of right thinking, in a truly Christian life. Anglican moral thinking since the seventeenth century has always taken into account the technicalities involved. The Bible does not, cannot provide answers to the moral questions that confront Christians today. Hard thinking by groups of competent men and women who themselves refuse to diminish human beings to the level of mere biological organisms is a Christian obligation.

Everything that has to do with human relationships is of the highest importance. That teaching lies at the heart of the Gospel. But working it out in a complex world such as ours calls for sound critical examination and responsible recommendation. The crucial question among all the many political and social questions is the true nature, meaning and destiny of human beings. Our Lord's command was that we should 'love God with all our heart, with all our soul, with all our mind, and with all our strength'. Loving God with all our mind in today's world is perhaps the most demanding of all the works of love. The experts do this on our behalf to help us to think more clearly about the real issues; but we also in our own way have to do our thinking as well, and decide where we stand.

Death is an awesome thing. Awesome because its onset is certain but unpredictable. It can be sudden or slow – the car crash or the long disease. It can come in old age or in youth. We feel differently about death in youth because death in old age comes as a natural event in a natural sequence. But it is always a tearing apart of relationships, a handing over of life and of all that makes life dear.

Fundamentally we need to acknowledge that death is natural. A human being differs from all other animals in his and her developed self-awareness, self-consciousness. A human being is a being who can without contradiction make two affirmations: 'I am' and 'I am to die'. However reluctant we are for most of our life to face the second affirmation I believe it to be an essential element in a person's maturity to be able to acknowledge the inevitability of death. I believe it to be one of the faults in our present culture that there seems almost a deliberate conspiracy of silence about this second affirmation, 'I am to die'. But to come to terms with the fact of one's own death greatly increases one's sense of the value of life, of the importance of time, of one's responsibility towards others – and, rightly taken, all this ministers not to gloom but to joy, not to self-centredness but to love.

Medical, biological, and scientific development has been so rapid and so sophisticated over the last half-century that remedies and procedures undreamt of three or four decades ago are now available. With these new procedures have come new moral dilemmas and ethical problems. That developments in surgery and chemotherapy should be raising *ethical* problems is in itself an important witness to the fact that even in this period of advanced science-based technology and secularised thinking there is still a widespread sense that there is something of crucial importance for civilised human existence in the distinction between *ought* and *ought not*. Still recognised, however dimly in some cases, is the mysterious sense of claim, of obligation.

As a result of a car accident John Jones is dying. As a result of some defect George Smith is in need of a heart transplant if he is to live. For a transplant to be effective it is important that only a certain period of time should elapse between the death of the donor and the operation on the receiver. Why should not the death of the dying donor be accelerated? On the answer you give to that question turns the whole question of the kind of being a human being is and the kind of behaviour that is appropriate and acceptable towards him.

There is at the root of our moral sensitivity and of our laws protecting human rights a conviction that a human being is a being towards whom we all have certain obligations. Among those obligations is the denial of freedom to the medical profession to accelerate death even for the advantage of another person's need.

In the field of medical ethics the ability to do something does not imply obligation to do it. *Can* does not imply *ought*. Whereas in the old ethical books we were taught – and rightly taught – that *ought* implies *can*, the doctor's dilemma in our time is more complex. He has more and more procedures at his disposal, but he has to assess his moral freedom to use some of these procedures in particular circumstances. The problem applies both to the issue of prolonging life and to the issue of accelerating death.

I once heard one of our most distinguished lawyers address an audience at the Royal Society of Medicine on the legal aspects of heart transplants. His essential point was that until the medical profession could clarify its procedure for certifying that death had taken place it was impossible for the law to provide adequate safeguards for the surgeon. As a layman in this area of responsibility I should like to say how sensitive I am to the burden of decision that the medical profession carries in this matter of life and death.

I can only approach this problem myself by regarding the sick person as the primary consideration. Whatever is to be done for the sick person must be done with full regard for that person's dignity and self-respect. But in addition to his unique personal identity and character he is also a person who relates to other persons who have regard and concern and affection for him – 'No man is an island'. So in facing the ethical dimension of therapy in cases of cancer we have somehow to relate scientific knowledge and capability with individual personal feelings, rights, and relationships.

At the present stage of scientific knowledge in this matter of cancerous conditions advances are being made all the time. Where a person is young, middle-aged, with others dependent upon him or her, I imagine that the desire of the patient, the patient's relations and the medical team will be to use whatever resources are available in the chemotherapy laboratory. But something of the pain of this kind of treatment I observed in the case of a former student of mine in his thirties who some ten years ago was dying of leukaemia and subjected to experiences in the name of therapy which – had they been withheld – would have enabled his dying to be less distressing for himself, for his wife and friends. At what cost in personal distress and indignity have we the right to subject a person to this kind of experimentation?

In this whole area of dilemma and concern I believe that Dame Cicely Saunders has presented us with a theory and a practice of exceptional sensitivity and importance. The theory and the practice are a marriage of sophisticated pain-control and nursing care with sympathetic personal and individual concern for the quality of the life that is left to the patient. Her book *The Management of Terminal Disease* dealt with the clinical aspects and was addressed to consultants and hospital doctors. Thereafter she edited *Hospice: The Living Idea*, a collection of essays from twenty-eight contributors and intended for all who are concerned with persons in terminal illness, not least for the family physician who occupies that most sensitive area of relationship between the dying person and the family.

Not all persons who are in need of this kind of care are able to receive it in spite of the remarkable spread of the idea and the number of centres now available. I do believe, however, that her approach, both scientific and human, and her experience can with great advantage become part of the fundamental thinking of all of us in this area of suffering and concern.

Underlying all this is I suppose a recognition that death is not an evil to be resisted at all costs. Death is essentially a stage in a natural process which has a beginning and a middle and an end.

Cicely Saunders argues that a human person should be helped to achieve his or her death. The aim of clinical medicine should be to achieve a tolerable threshold of pain and so to give the maximum freedom to the person to face, come to terms with his or her dying, and move peacefully into it.

I suppose it would be possible to arrive at a complicated scientific formula which would satisfy the scientist's understanding of the word 'health'. I doubt if it would be possible to arrive at a comparable scientific formula which would be an equivalent for the word 'happiness'.

There are those individuals who seem able to achieve a degree of happiness while being in a state of un-health. Health and happiness are not equivalents. But they have this much in common. Aristotle defined happiness as a state of well-being that supervenes upon activity in which an individual is confidently engaged – as when a master carpenter is shaping wood for a particular purpose. I want to suggest that health also indicates a state of well-being that supervenes upon activity, attitudes, relationships that are, for want of a better word, 'right' for that person. Health is an experience which supervenes when we live appropriately in relationship with God, with our environment, with other people, with ourself. In science health is a word capable of being defined in a formula; in religion health is seen rather as a consequence of spirituality – if by spirituality we mean relationships which involve both interior attitudes and exterior actions.

As I understand it, Christianity is a way of dancing to the music of time – which music is both the heard melodies of everyday experience and the secret harmonies of God. The Gospel is the good news that there are these secret harmonies of God interpenetrating the heard melodies of everyday circumstance and personal temperament. Grace, we are told, is given to perfect nature.

Our great need is to reaffirm in our secularised culture the dimensions of transcendence, spirituality, and community. The way we are with others is all bound up with the way we are with ourselves: the way we are with ourselves is all bound up with the way we are with others: the way we are with others and the way we are with ourselves is all bound up with the way we are with God: and the way we are with God is all bound up with the way we are with the Holy Spirit of God who takes the things concerning Jesus and reveals them to us afresh in succeeding generations and in each succeeding day. The appointed time is always here and now.

A priest does not spend his time looking for appreciation, but there are times when he feels an odd man out amid the changing values of modern society. He feels sometimes that he is the man nobody knows: in our modern society Christ and the Church and all that the Church stands for have been pushed to the outer edges of the nation's expectations. To be a committed Christian nowadays, to be a man or woman of faith and prayer, is to be unusual. All Christians, not only priests, share in the feeling of being the odd man out, the man nobody knows. Unless we can interpret this in relation to Christ who was rejected and crucified, unless we can use this experience to identify ourselves more imaginatively with the millions of the world's poor, the world's homeless, the world's underfed, unless we can see our situation as Christians in relation to Christ crucified and humanity suffering we shall be tempted to give up the struggle and sink back into the easy mediocrity of indifference. But relate your sense of isolation and your doubts to Christ and you will be saved from the temptation to opt out. Instead you will see what you experience as isolation as part of the experience of Christ; and you will understand the experience of Christ as the evidence that God suffers in the life of the world he loves.

A good old age is something we each have to achieve – to prepare for, work at – so that in our declining years we are a burden neither to ourselves nor to our children, nor to those on whose kindness and service we shall increasingly depend. Learning to 'grow old gracefully' is a Christian possibility and a Christian duty. It means letting go of all regrets about growing old, letting go all resentment that we can no longer do all the things we used to do. It means accepting our present state of life without complaint. It means keeping ourselves open to God and to Christ in worship and prayer.

When we are younger and active we have to learn to let God into all our *activities*. As we grow older we have to learn to let God into all our *passivities* – all our diminishments. Accepting these diminishments – our loss of vitality and energy, of sight and hearing – requires a deliberate choice and decision. Old age is something to be achieved, not something to be regretted. Determine to make something of your declining years.

It helps if we refuse to allow our thoughts to dwell on the painful experiences of our past life. We need to purge our memory. One way to do this is to make an honest confession and acknowledgement of our past sins and wrongdoings. Face what we feel guilty about, face what we have done and are now ashamed of having done – bring it all up to the surface and tell it all out to God our Father and receive the assurance that all this is forgiven; and then forget it, let it go. We need to purge our memory of all that troubles us so that we can receive from God his deep gift of peace.

It also helps us if we refuse to allow our thoughts to dwell in anxiety or in fear of what the future may have in store for us. We need to learn not to be afraid of dying, not to be afraid of death. We all must die, since dying is a necessary part of living. St Francis, when he was dying, added another verse to his Canticle of the Sun in which he praised God for all his gifts in nature and human nature and supremely his gift of Christ. This is what he wrote: 'Praise to God for Sister Death'.

What lies beyond death we cannot know. We have to pass beyond death before we shall know what there is to be known.

But for those of us who are Christians there is already the knowledge that we have a relationship here and now already with one who is himself beyond death. For we believe that Jesus who was crucified, dead, and buried is a living, if unseen, presence within the community of faith. We have his words to prepare us for a continuing relationship beyond death with one who already beyond death is in relationship with us now. 'Because I live, you shall live also.' 'In my Father's house are many rooms – I go to prepare a place for you.'

We cannot imagine what God is like – but we can believe that God is like Jesus. Hold on to the Christlikeness of God. Have faith that God is love and that God's love comes to us from the other side of death.

To help us to become more aware of God and more trustful of God, we should call to mind often the many good things we have enjoyed in our long lives. Think on the good things and the joyful things and the beautiful things – remember them often, call them to mind and let them increase your gratitude, your thankfulness. Few things can better help us to grow old gracefully than to increase our sense of gratitude and thankfulness. Gratitude will lead us to see ever more clearly that life is a gift – not something we have made ourselves, but always something given, not a possession to clutch to ourselves, but a gift we have received, and a gift to be handed over at the end.

We hand ourselves over as we are, as we have made ourselves in the course of our years, as we have become. To die is to hand back to our Father his gift of life as we have shaped it and used it and made it out of the raw material of our circumstances, out of the sorrows and the joys, the failures and the achievements of our years. As Jesus on the cross handed himself over to his Father – so let us learn to live and grow old so that at the end we can say: 'Father, into thy hands I commend my spirit.'

> Man is made for joy and woe,
> And if this we rightly know
> Thro' the world we safely go.
> Joy and woe are woven fine
> A clothing for the soul divine.

'It is such an all-enveloping experience which utterly changes every aspect of life.' So wrote a woman whose progress through a bereavement seven years ago, leaving her with five children of school age, I have been able in a small way to share. She goes on:

> God has made a world in which catastrophes do occur; people do die, often unexpectedly, often unnaturally young, but this is part of the world we live in and in the natural order of things. God allows it to happen but does not *will* it for the individual. This has been of the greatest comfort to me in accepting my husband's death . . . For those of us with children it is essential to try to help them to accept life and death as natural things even if we cannot understand the timing. To this end I believe it is important to talk about the person who has died and to try not to allow home life to be robbed of its essential ingredients, love and gaiety and fun.

Sometimes, as at the end of a long and weary illness, death comes with an element of relief and thankfulness woven into the awfulness of the separation, the sheer physical absence and emptiness. At other times the unexpectedness, the suddenness, the outrage hits you, stuns you, produces the physical symptoms of shock. Even if you have been expecting the end you find yourself unprepared for the end when it comes. And when it comes the first feeling is the sense of no feeling, of numbness, of blunting. Often this numbness is broken with outbursts of anger and distress. Anxiety and emotional pain sometimes bring with them physical discomforts and illness. These symptoms together with the most intense emotional distress gradually pass and give way to long-continuing but changing experiences of yearning, of searching, of restlessness, of feeling he is here – here and yet not here. Pangs of intense grief become less intense after a few weeks but can always be re-aroused by some unexpected reminder.

The experience of bereavement will always be personal to each individual even if some rhythm is to be detected in most people as they journey through grief. A woman who has had a very dependent relationship over many years with her husband has invested so much of herself in this relationship that she loses a wide segment of her life space and she feels completely mutilated. 'I feel that my heart has been torn out.' 'I feel I've shrunk.' Where the relationship of husband and wife has been less close, more ambivalent, two people at odds, where each has had some sort of wish that something would happen to end it, the death of one can leave the other not elated but depressed and guilty.

Each bereaved person will react differently according to the character of the relationship that has been ended and his own personality and temperament. But to every bereaved person it can be said: 'You should not hide your grief or suppress your emotions or pretend not to be suffering'. Grief is a process that has to be worked through – the more fully and freely the better; and at no other period of life is it more helpful to have a friend who understands, who can listen, to whom one can speak all that one feels.

Shakespeare understood human emotions as well as any man and his advice is sound:

> Give sorrow words, the grief that does not speak
> Whispers the o'er-fraught heart and bids it break.

The loss of security, the sense of outrage, the weight of responsibility, the burden of having to make all the decisions, the needs of the children when your heart is dry and you feel only a deep inner emptiness and lack of any desire to live – all this can produce for a time deep feelings of rage and hostility against the hospital, the doctor, the parish priest, against God. 'Why did he have to die?' 'Why did God take him away so young?'

Other people, relatives, friends are often embarrassed by a person's bereavement, afraid of another person's emotions and suffering, anxious to keep a sufficient emotional distance, driven sometimes to say clumsy and unintentionally hurtful things. To reassure themselves they are quick to commend the bereaved person's courage: 'How well you have got over it', they say after six months. But a bereaved person has never 'got over it' after six months; the grieving process goes on at different levels for years and this is where the really understanding friend is such a support. 'Be open to other people's help,' writes my correspondent. 'It is a great temptation to shut oneself away. Don't be afraid to share your feelings with someone who really cares. It takes courage to let down the barriers and to be open and to speak of the pain and bewilderment, but to allow another to share in this is healing'.

Some people are tempted to cherish and prolong their unhappiness, to dwell too much on the past. But we must live today and tomorrow. Bereavement is an experience we cannot escape: it must be faced and coped with using whatever resources are at hand – the friendship of those who care; the maintaining of former associations; worship with one's fellow Christians however acutely you may experience your isolation; prayer even if you only cry your grief; social activities even though you feel other people are self-consciously trying to make you feel at home.

A doctor of wide experience has written:

> Grief itself I see as a process of realisation, the process by which we make real inside us an event that has already occurred outside of us. It's as if throughout our life we're building up a picture of the world, a set of plans and assumptions about the world. And as long as these remain constant, we go happily along from day to day. When something happens which quite suddenly removes a whole set of plans, a whole set of expectations, a very large section of our world, we're left with a gap. I see grief as the psychological process by which people fill that gap. Because it is a process, that's to say something occurring over time and something which changes its nature, it has a history, it passes through different phases.

The numbness, yearning and disorganisation have to be suffered, endured, accepted. But what is desirable for health and for happiness is the gradual embracing of a phase of reorganisation when new aims and new interests are taken up. This phase of reorientation purposefully and positively towards the future will be experienced differently and achieved differently according to each person's circumstances and temperament and resources of courage and of friends.

It is at this point especially that the whole community of the nation with its welfare provisions as well as the local community of neighbourhood and Church have as yet not fully recognised responsibilities and opportunities. Help can be offered so clumsily that more harm is done than good. But real help is needed if a widow is to be able to accept herself in her new condition as one who is fully accepted by friends and neighbours and made to feel that she matters and that life has meaning and her own life has purpose.

If she has within herself resources of faith in the reality of God and in the grace and help that comes through prayer and sacrament, then she will have from this faith enormous help in making this deep readjustment in hope. Even if she does not have such personal faith she cannot but be greatly helped in making this transition into a new way of life if she finds among the local Christian community friends who quietly and sensitively draw her into their company.

Dependent children can help a widow in working her way through grief to a reorganisation of her life precisely because they are dependent and need her care. But she will be all the more vulnerable because they will remind her of her loss and solitude, and will sometimes work out their own grief and bewilderment on her, offering not affection and understanding but aloofness and resistance. A widow has to understand not only her own grief but her children's grief. Each child will be affected differently. If she looks for an understanding of her own grief from her children and seeks consolation there, she is likely not to find it, to be further hurt in consequence and the children made even more insecure. But if in her own grief she can make the greater effort to try to understand their grief, she will be able to help them and be herself helped in helping them. The sheer fact of their existence, their deprivation and need will draw out from her love and concern in spite of her own inner feeling of emptiness and loss of power to love.

We shall experience terrible loneliness. But there is always somewhere someone to whom we can open our grief and with whom we can share our sorrow. To the bereaved I would say, 'Seek a friend who is strong enough to stand with you during your progress towards a new reorganisation of your life'. I recall the obligation implicit in words of St James – the obligation to become such persons as are able to stand with the bereaved and succour them in their distress with sensitive, understanding love. What St James has written for the Church of all subsequent ages is: 'True religion is this: to help the widowed and fatherless in their affliction'.

I am not really sure what people mean when they talk about being saved. Sometimes they seem to use the word of a situation from which a person may need to be rescued. But this is not the chief meaning of the words 'save' and 'salvation' in the New Testament. There the emphasis is positive. 'Salvation' is a word which speaks about man's true life – about a quality of wholeness, of health, which is given to human life when it is being lived in a right relation to God and to other people through God. It may be through meeting a person whose life radiates this quality that we come to know that we need to be made whole ourselves. More often, however, we reach this knowledge by a different route. Something goes wrong and we find we cannot blame anybody else. The unwelcome thought strikes us that maybe the source of the trouble is in ourselves. Life loses its sweetness: we feel bored perhaps, or unwanted.

If I look at my own experience or the experience of others who have talked to me, I know that there are certain states of mind, certain misunderstandings, certain fixed attitudes, from which we need to be rescued if we are to be fully effective. It is when we have unresolved inner conflicts, when we are blind and lack self-awareness, that we are vulnerable in ourselves and sometimes very difficult for others to live with. But it may need some kind of crisis or collapse before we see that this is how things are with us, that we need to be 'saved'.

How we can achieve salvation seems to depend a great deal on holy luck – on meeting the right person at the right time. For the most part we are helped towards a fuller, freer life by other people, by the touch of another life on our own. Much depends on the persons who happen to be our parents, schoolteachers, friends, parish priests, workmates; or the chance meetings – the stranger met on holiday, the nurse who looked after us in hospital. Something in them touches something in us, and we see ourselves in a new light; new possibilities open up. Very often these people – these healers, we might call them – would themselves express their debt to others who have touched their lives. And in this touching again and again you find Christ, you find God. You find that they believe in God, that for them Christ is their standard of what a human being should be and, more than that, the person from whose life they draw their own resources.

What I understand by being set free is something more than becoming psychologically adjusted, even if some people need the help of psychotherapists to sort out their emotional tangles before they can respond to the touch of Christ. But this 'something more' is a kind of vision of higher possibilities of personal development – of relationships at a deeper level of love and trust. Once you see this as possible and desirable, you come alive to a new sense of what it can mean to be a person. And help is available. If you have the courage to pierce through the often unattractive outer crust of the Church community, you will find that it has a warm centre where there is much understanding love and the capacity to set us free from whatever it is that shuts us off from wholeness.

And if we fail? If God is God – and nobody can prove that God is not – then I can see no reason for thinking that my death ends my relationship with God. And if God is asking me through Christ here and now to make a certain kind of response – of faith and obedience and love – then I cannot see how my relationship to God after death can be unaffected by the way I behave in my relationship to God now: and relationship to God includes relationship to other people.

If I am to use the words 'heaven' and 'hell', then for me they are symbols which stand for two ways of knowing God: 'heaven' means knowing God in the exchange of love; 'hell' means knowing God as the love you have rejected. We experience something of heaven now, and something, too, of hell. Sartre said, 'Hell is other people'; T S Eliot said, 'Hell is oneself.' It is from hell now – in the sense of miserable preoccupation with ourselves, self-enclosure, self-exclusion from the fuller life – that we need to be rescued. And then perhaps we can become rescuers of others.

Even those people who do not find it possible to believe in Jesus the Christ in the ways that we Christians believe in him, must, if they are prepared to read the Gospels, acknowledge that Jesus was remembered as a teller of incomparable short stories.

Those stories were remembered and retold again and again by his friends so that they were fixed in the memory of the first Christians in the sort of way that nursery rhymes and folk tales are fixed in the memory of every child who has the good luck to have parents who understand the importance of feeding a child's imagination. But the stories Jesus told were told to adults. They are factual, told with an economy of words and a vividness of expression. And they are told in order to open the imagination of the hearers to see more deeply into the meaning of the life they are already living. Such is the wonderful power of the story: it works on the imagination, it awakens new awareness of the way things are.

One of the best known of the Jesus stories is the one we refer to as 'The Prodigal Son'. The label is misleading. The key person in the story is the father, not the sons; and the elder brother as well as the younger is essential to the story. Be that as it may, look at the story in terms of *responses*: the response of the younger son to his home situation and his desire to leave home for the wider world outside; the response of the father to the younger son's request – his willingness to let him go; the response of the younger son to the actual experience of poverty to which he was reduced as a result of squandering his patrimony – that marvellous phrase, 'And when he came to himself'; the response of the father to the returning son; the response of the elder brother to the way the father had responded to the returning younger son; the response of the father to his elder son's response.

In this story there is nothing sick about these responses. The younger son's desire to explore the wider world is commendable, as is the willingness of the father to let him go. The elder son's response to the father's welcome to the returning boy is understandable. Both sons in their different ways acted immaturely. The only one of the three who was fully in control was the father. The pain he personally suffered became in him the power of a love that reconciled. Let his responses teach you whatever there is in them that you need to see and assimilate for your own soul's health.

The father in this story Jesus told is surely to be understood by us as an image of God, an expression in human terms of that

Divine Other to whom Jesus prayed and taught us to pray – addressing God as 'Father'. But you and I are made in the image of God. The whole point of this Christianity of ours is that we shall cooperate with God in allowing this Godlikeness to find expression in the way we live, the way we are with ourselves, the way we respond to others.

Consider two inadequate ideas of God which develop in childhood and which must be changed if the adult is to be able to have a genuine relationship to God. First, the child experts tell us that there is a tendency in childhood to split experience into good and bad and to identify good experience with an idealised parent figure. A child will prefer to think that his mother is perfect. He will feel more secure that way. Later when it becomes impossible to believe any longer that his mother is perfect he will tend to project the idealised parent idea on to God. The common idea of God as loving and kind but unable to do anything effective about the difficult, harsh side of life results in this way. The idea of God so formed is an inadequate one and will tend to lead a man to see God behind only half his experience, that experience which seems to him good. But the real God is behind all his experience, not only what he feels to be good but also what he feels to be bad.

Another inadequate idea of God is the stern repressive father idea. The root of this idea of God lies in the child's tendency to identify part of itself with the commands and prohibitions given by parents and others in authority. Freud calls that part of ourselves that agrees with these voices of authority the 'super-ego'. It is a kind of internal policeman who makes you feel guilty if you disobey the standards of behaviour that society inculcates through the agency of parents and teachers. This super-ego is not infrequently read into the idea of God, so that you feel God to be a kind of accuser and judge combined. But the real God is behind not only the voices of authority but also our instinctive rebellion against them. He is the creator and redeemer of the whole of us.

The Bible recognises that there are true and false ideas of God. You have only to call to mind the scorn of the Prophet

Isaiah's attack on false gods – false gods in the mind, not only those made of wood and stone. In the First Epistle of St John we hear the argument that if a man says that he loves God and actually hates his brother he is a liar. The man St John has in mind is a man who really thinks he does love God; but his attitude to his brother proves him to be mistaken. His mistake perhaps arises from identifying an idea of God which he finds personally reassuring with God himself. But God is not an idea. He is a living power who is addressing him through his brother.

To uncover falsehood and to disclose truth is surely one of the most necessary of all human duties if civilised behaviour is to be protected and developed. Not for nothing is the Devil called the father of lies.

At one level the courts of law, at another level academic institutions, at another level the home and family are places where civilised behaviour is protected and developed. Father and mother, unless they abdicate from one of their highest responsibilities, are the guardians of truth in the inner mind and soul of their children. A family interrogation can be very painful, but every exposure of the lie is a victory in the battle for truth. At this level then, interrogation is an expression of love. A child needs to experience love in two dimensions – the one unconditional, the other conditional. To experience love as unconditional is a fundamental human need. The child needs to know that whatever happens, whatever he may do, he will never lose his parents' acceptance of him as their son. But the child also needs to know what are the boundaries of acceptable behaviour, and often the parent and the child find themselves locked in a painful interrogation when those boundaries have been overstepped. Love demands discipline, for true love is concern for the true wellbeing of the other. Love's painful conditions are made tolerable only when the unconditional fundamental acceptance of child by parent is recognised by both.

Our Christianity, our Christian understanding of the meaning of being alive and being human, is all bound up with those two dimensions of love. For that reason Christian experience is frequently the experience of interrogation. Our innermost self is searched by the questions at the heart of the Gospel and the Church. If you don't want your innermost self to be searched, then keep away from the Gospel and the Church. And if you do allow yourself to become involved in the life of the Church, be prepared to be interrogated in your inmost soul by the Gospel.

Who, would you say, is in the worse case: the person who recognises the demands that Christianity will make if he opens his life to its claims, and so decides to have nothing to do with it; or the person who involves himself with Christianity and fails to admit and respond to the claims being made on his life? And which of us is not in one way or another resisting some of the claims which are the conditions of the unconditional love of God?

For the most part Christianity interrogates us, individually and as a community, by an indirect rather than by a direct method. In all our gatherings for worship we listen to extracts being read from that strange but persisting anthology of ancient writings we call the Bible. We listen to the readings as in some way addressed to us and intended in some way to cause us to think new thoughts or to think old thoughts afresh or at a deeper level. Such is the content of these scripture readings that for all their strangeness and remoteness they do, if we really attend, address us here and now. Often what we hear read is a story about other people, and if we attend to the story with mind and heart open to receive it, we shall usually find ourselves being drawn into it and searched by it.

Indeed, the whole Bible is a kind of continuation in a variety of forms and occasions of that primal interrogation in the opening chapter of Genesis. Adam, the symbol of mankind, has eaten of the forbidden fruit which has opened his eyes to a different understanding of the way things are; he is terrified by the new knowledge born of disobedience as he hides himself with Eve when he becomes aware of God calling him: 'Adam, where art thou?' I believe that this interrogation goes to the deep centre of our being and of our behaviour. God searches us to declare ourselves: 'Man, where are you? On what are you setting your heart? What are the values by which you are guiding your life?' Sometimes in the Old Testament this interrogation searches the soul of an individual, like David in the matter of Bathsheba, sometimes the allegiance of the nation, like Israel in the matter of treaty negotiations with Egypt. Yet all this interrogation is sharpened in the story that has Jesus at the centre, the stories that he told in order to open men's eyes to the truth and the story of his own life and its relationships with friends and foes, his silence under the interrogation of the Roman Governor and his acceptance of crucifixion. Jesus is our interrogator now because he was found in full integrity under the interrogation of his contemporaries.

Jesus confronts us through the reading of the Gospels in our worship as the embodiment of a love that is unconditional and a love that makes conditions. We are enabled to accept the conditions because we believe that they are the conditions laid on us by the one who above all others is our friend, who desires nothing else but our greatest good, the utter integrity of our soul, our union with him and through him with the Father, his Father and our Father, the God who is all Love.

No Christian can be complacent about the future of Christianity in these islands. Our faith will give us confidence that the truth of Christianity is great and that it will prevail. As John Buchan once wrote: 'Christianity is an anvil that has worn out many hammers.' But today we are not experiencing hammer blows so much as a more insidious erosion due to neglect, indifference, inability to see that what Christianity stands for is important for the health of the nation and the happiness of individuals. There is nothing in our situation to allow us to be complacent.

The future of Christianity in these islands will depend increasingly on the number and quality of Christian men and women in education, primary, secondary and tertiary in schools and colleges. The abdication of many parents from their responsibility towards their children and the breaking down of former ties between children and local parish and congregation are two factors alone that make it necessary in these days for the teacher in the schools to be something of a parent and something of a priest towards the nation's children, as well as being their teacher.

Whether we consider the use we have been making of our Church schools or whether we consider the use we have been making of our legal standing in the schools of the state, we can none of us be complacent about the effectiveness of what we have been doing. There are, of course, excellent teachers who through religious instruction periods communicate not merely information but a vision of what it means to be a new man in Christ. When interviewing candidates for theological courses in a university, I not infrequently discovered that what has turned a young man or a young woman's thoughts towards the study of theology has been the influence on them of one of their teachers at school. But taken by and large too often the teaching of the Christian tradition has been dull, unintelligent, unrelated to experience and in its effect often positively harmful, leaving children with a hatred of the Bible and a rejection of what it stands for.

Not only is there no cause for complacency about the use we are making of our present opportunities, there is a mounting criticism of what is called the Christian monopoly in this field. If we are to meet this criticism creatively, we must not only do much better what we are already trying to do; we must also come out to meet these others who are concerned about the moral education of children and see if we cannot achieve a co-operation of the goodwill and concern of humanist teachers with ourselves.

The main issue is not the best way of giving Christian instruction in schools. The main issue is how Christians in education can help all children and all students to come to an adequate understanding of life as it is and as it could be. Christians in education are not simply concerned to spread the knowledge of Christianity. We are concerned with the whole range of education. Our prior concern is for truth, for dispelling ignorance, for opening up new horizons so that children and young people can come to an adequate understanding of life as it is. This means mathematics, and science, and literature, and music; this means the training of the interpretative structures of the mind; the awakening of sensitivities. In this we are at one with all who are concerned with education but are motivated by humanist and humanitarian rather than avowedly Christian impulses.

Christians working together with humanists must press for more adequate national policies so that all schools may be made as good as the best are now, so that all children may have the opportunity to grow to their full stature, so that society at large may carry on the good work of the schools and not stultify it. As it is, teachers have in some cases to battle with all kinds of influences in home and neighbourhood which undermine what they are trying to do.

If education is not just a matter of learning but rather a matter of learning to live, the children need more than an adequate understanding of life as it is; they need to have their eyes opened to life as it ought to be, as it could be. This means education in moral and spiritual and social values; this means facing questions about the experiences and problems of being a person. Such questions are raised no less by the five-year-old whose pet kitten has been run over than by the sixteen-year-old whose close friend has been killed in a road accident. At all ages and stages the young have moral problems, relationship problems, questions and perplexities and doubts.

Not only humanist but Christian teachers also are questioning whether the moral and religious education offered in secondary schools is an adequate interpretation of life as the child experiences it or an adequate preparation for life in years ahead. In a nation where the Christian faith and Christian presuppositions cannot be taken for granted any more, it may paradoxically be dangerous if moral and social and spiritual values are exclusively bound up with the teaching of the Bible. The rejection of religious faith may mean the rejection of moral and personal values also.

Modern psychology is teaching us a great deal about the emotional needs of children. Teaching about the Bible, teaching about the Christian faith and life needs to be integrated into a more open approach to moral education. But this teaching needs to be child-centred and not simply historical; helping children to interpret their own experience rather than burdening their memories with ancient history.

Even so the past matters. In a nation whose culture and customs have been significantly shaped by Christian influences, it is surely vital that new generations shall be put in contact with their own cultural roots. An agnostic headmaster saw this clearly enough when he insisted on improving the teaching of religion in his school as a necessary part of preparing children to understand English literature and history. On social, cultural and, therefore, psychological grounds alone the case for continuing Christian education in state schools can be powerfully argued. But this very fact makes it all the more urgent for Christian educationalists to explore new and better ways of presenting Christianity.

Education is not just a matter of learning but of learning to live, of learning to live well. What counts as preparation for life is not just the curriculum but the character of the school; not just the competence but the character of the teacher. If God is to be God in the sphere of education then it is not merely the quality of what is taught which will awaken awareness, but much more the child's contact with teachers whose lives communicate Christ's presence because of what they are themselves becoming – by virtue of the fact that they are always keeping themselves open to Christ, open to God.

There is a familiar prayer in which we are invited to pray that we may so pass through things temporal that we finally lose not the things eternal. I do not understand this prayer only as making a distinction between life before death and life after death. 'Temporal' and 'eternal' are for me indicators of the two dimensions in which we live and move and have all our being. These words point to the same contrast and the same interpenetration as the Pauline words flesh and spirit. We only understand ourselves rightly when we understand ourselves as embodied spirits. The energies of the spirit are not imprisoned within the cage of the flesh. The energies of the spirit penetrate the flesh and illuminate it and enable things eternal to become active within things temporal. This is the principle of incarnation. The word was made flesh, and in the flesh of time and history, in the actual circumstances of an actual historical existence, this word which is God's word was translated from the language of eternity into the language of time. We can read this story for ourselves in the four Gospels and we can measure its transfiguring effect in the letters of Paul and Peter and John.

So in our world today in which humankind everywhere seems to be behaving like sheep without a shepherd, we are to pray that we may so live our lives that we do not lose the things eternal – the values, the spirituality, and the practical care and compassion for those in need which are the hallmarks of the Christ-life.

If there is any meaning in this mystery of being alive and being human, if this self-awareness with all its pain and all its joy which forms the unique central experience of each one of us adds up to anything finally fulfilling, we are not able to know while we are still in temporal flesh. Such light as we have – and it is enough light to support us in faith – is the glory of God in the face of Jesus Christ and in the faces of all manner of nameless men and women who so handle the given circumstances of this life that we can have no doubt that they have not lost the things eternal.

If you ask yourself the seemingly simple question, 'Who is a Christian?' you will not find it easy to give an equally simple answer. The meaning of the word 'Christian' is not simple and straightforward. It is a bit like the word 'gentleman' which in the eighteenth century described a man at a certain level in the social scale, a man of property without any reference to character or conduct. Today it is a word with a moral implication. Originally men and women in the ancient world were called Christian in respect of their membership of an identifiable group – the company of the followers of Christ. Christian was a label, almost a nickname. Latterly the words 'Christian' or 'un-Christian' have become adjectives with reference to character or conduct.

Then, to make confusion worse, we find the word 'Christian' attached in some countries to a political party – for instance, Christian Democrats. It is presumably possible to be a Moslem and belong to the party of Christian Democrats. More bizarre still, massacres in Beirut were carried out by members of the Christian Phalange. So *who* is a Christian?

Among the city lights of Piccadilly Circus there was a famous circular advertisement for Coca Cola. All was dark and then from the centre rapidly in concentric circles the electric bulbs flashed on, adding circle upon circle out to the circumference. Then they all went out and the operation began again. If you think of the centre of that circle as the living Christ, then each of the widening circles can be said to represent different degrees of relationship between individual Christians and Christ.

There are those near the centre who have reached a clear conviction that where Christ is and what Christ stands for is where they wish to be. In intention and in practice – as far as they can – the primary loyalty of their lives is to Christ and his teaching as the life-option they have chosen. Such people have made a choice out of all possible options: 'I am for Christ'. It is from such persons that the martyrs of all ages have been drawn. Under pressure of circumstances at the ultimate point of decision, they have stood firm for Christ and have been ready to pay for that choice with their lives.

Those who in faith and prayer seek to stand where Christ stands, and to give themselves so to live that Christ may live in them and through them touch the lives of others, are the most deeply aware of the distance between what they are and what they have not yet allowed themselves to become. Not *pride* at being close to Christ but *penitence* for being still so far from expressing a true likeness to Christ. Penitence, not pride, will be the inner attitude of true Christians.

At a further remove from the centre will be the wider circle of those whose understanding of the claims of Christ does not draw them within the worshipping community of faith and prayer – or perhaps only occasionally. Christ for them means a certain style or standard of behaviour and relationship. They would wish to be known as Christians in terms of the values to which they subscribe and the standards they wish to uphold and teach their children. Many of these people are most generous of their time in promoting good causes and serving human needs. The concept of Christ as the servant will perhaps be at the heart of their understanding of Christ and of what it means to be a Christian. These persons are the salt of the earth and human life would be harsher for us all without them. They believe in the concept and practice of service as one of the fundamental necessities of civilised living.

Further out in the widening circles of those who draw something of the light by which they live from Christian sources are those who care about speaking truth, about dealing honestly in business, about being kind and not being cruel – but whose outlook, standards, attitude, are not very open to new thoughts about the way they live or the quality of their relationships. These people have no relationship with the community of worshipping Christians, no clear knowledge of Christ, but perhaps a lingering feeling for something beyond themselves which is vaguely connected with the word 'God'.

That advertisement light I remember in Piccadilly Circus was a light that sprang out of darkness and moved out into darkness in circles further and further away from the source of the electric impulse. And so I suspect it has always been for nearly 2,000 years. Christian qualities have been communicated from the bright centre of those who have given themselves to be lights of Christ in the succeeding generations in ever-widening circles and have sustained men and women with hope and courage in grim situations.

We cannot ourselves solve all the massive problems of the world but we can live and pray and act out our Christian beliefs about what it means to be alive and human at such a time as this – facing the difficulties and the near-despair but so trusting in the love of God in spite of all appearances to the contrary that we are able to address ourselves honestly to the question of what we really believe to be the truth about God, the truth about Christ, the truth about prayer, the truth about living Christianly. Why am I trying to live as a Christian and what does it require of me to live as a Christian? These questions will uncover our own doubts and uncertainties. But truth must be our aim. For only truth can set us free really to live a whole and happy and creative life.

How little we really know on our wedding day of the stresses and strains that our deeper emotional personalities will cause us to suffer under the pressures of the changing circumstances of family and job and getting older, and the impact of other people's presence on one or other of us – or on both. To marry is indeed to take in hand an enterprise that is not without risk.

Perhaps that is why a number of our sons and daughters have chosen to live together without getting married.

How important it is, therefore, that young people should be helped to avoid false, romantic, sentimental expectations of what married life is all about. How necessary it is for all of us to learn and re-learn that a husband must accept his wife afresh each day and a wife her husband. We do change. The enterprise will be under great strain sometimes, and one of the essential safeguards or tie-bars of the structure is what I call mutual acceptance daily renewed: 'I John take thee Joan today – twenty, forty years after – as I know you *now*'. And mutual acceptance daily renewed is another way of saying mutual forgiveness daily renewed. Forgiveness, acceptance, repentance, tolerance, openness – these are some of the ingredients surely of the kind of love which has the power to keep in balance two persons through all the strains and stresses of this demanding enterprise which for all its difficulties is full of the possibility of deepest joy and glowing happiness.

Husband and wife need to be constantly watchful of their relationship, careful to keep their relationship in repair, studying to be open with each other about everything, about their inner hurts and anxieties as well as about the practical decisions which the family enterprise requires to be made; really listening to each other, listening no less to their children.

If you ask me to speak of this love less obliquely and more directly, let me say this. The constant love that is needed for the enterprise of married life and family life is self-forgetful concentration on the true well-being of the other.

There are three kinds of loving in this togetherness. All three are needed. There is the erotic love, the original attraction, the mutual exploration and joy of sexual relationship. And this erotic loving calls for our best attention. How often a marriage relationship dies because the sexual play is not properly understood or sensitively enacted. Intercourse becomes no more than a sexual release, and all its human and personal pleasurableness is diminished because the art of this kind of loving is not attended to with sufficient care.

Erotic love is not enough to hold together a marriage and keep in balance the thrust and counterthrust of two personalities who for all that they are 'one flesh' remain separate persons. Erotic love itself needs the other kind of loving, that self-forgetful concentration on the true well-being of the other. That kind of loving for which the New Testament word is *agape* – the kind of loving which can best be described as the 'Christ kind' of loving. These, then, are two of the loves needed for the togetherness of marriage – *agape* and *eros*, *eros* and *agape*. Erotic relationship and agapeistic relationship – in which the Christ kind of loving helps the sexual kind of loving to be a joyful exchange between two persons rather than a mere biological release of sexual energy.

There is a third kind of loving which perhaps becomes more important as we get older: *philia* – friendship, companionship. For husband and wife to be friends, to enjoy doing things together as friends do enjoy each other's company, is a lovely thing to observe. It needs interests in common outside the enterprise of marriage and family so that companionship and conversation is kept alive and fresh. But here again the deep secret of true friendship is its Christ-centredness, so movingly expressed in a Latin lyric of the ninth century:

> Christ who first gave thee for a friend to me,
> Christ keep thou well, where're thou art, for me . . .
> And God, who brought us on this earth together,
> Bring us together in His house of heaven.

Together in love. There is no human enterprise more demanding or more rewarding; more exposed to pain, more creative of pleasure. The way we live and love together as husband and wife rubs off on our children. It is from what we are together that they will catch both style and confidence for their own adventure in relationships. But nothing in this enterprise is automatic or guaranteed. At all times we must watch over it, guard its inner silences and solitudes, keep it open to others and fresh in the range of its interests. Such watchfulness demands that we each – husband and wife – keep watch over our inner thoughts, attitudes, anxieties, resentments, disappointments, desires.

This kind of watchfulness belongs at the centre of being a true inward Christian.

Watch and pray is a frequent word to us of the Christ. Watch and pray that you may go forward into the unknown of the future together in the three loves, with courage and hope, knowing that whatever happens there is always a creative and a loving thing to do.

W. S. Gilbert wrote that

> Every boy and every girl
> That's born into this world alive
> Is either a little Liberal
> Or else a little Conservative.

The accident of birth gives a particular shape to all our lives and influences our outlook. I was born into the Church of England by the accident of birth and the convictions of my parents. I might have been born a Methodist or a Roman Catholic. But I am an Anglican now not just because of this accident of birth, baptism and upbringing, but by choice and conviction – and with immense gratitude.

The past history of the Christian Church in England matters to me. The long span of time past dwarfs us; it puts us in our place; it helps us to see things in perspective; it rebukes our preoccupation with our own importance or anxieties; we are made to think of what we owe to those who have lived before us. I find it both humbling and exhilarating to be the 77th Dean of Salisbury and to know that others will come after me on that long list of names on the south choir aisle screen which begins with the date 1091. The psalmist has written, 'The lot is fallen unto me in a fair ground: and so I have a goodly heritage'. A heritage is not something we fashion for ourselves; it is something handed on to us as a gift, a gift we have neither earned nor merited, but a gift of which we can at least try to be worthy.

Our worship here reminds us of the long-continuing witness of the Catholic Church and of our Anglican claim to be the continuing holy Catholic and Apostolic Church of all the ages in these islands – the accredited steward to the English people of those same mysteries of God which have sustained the generations that have gone before us. There is a particular richness and responsibility in our Anglican inheritance. For I believe that a better understanding of our past leads to a better understanding of our present and enables us to give ourselves as a Church to God for his fullest use of us in the future.

Among the great glories of our heritage are the ancient parish churches and cathedrals which for centuries have uplifted men's minds and hearts to God. We should visit these ancient churches whenever we can. It is good to allow the sense of history to possess us, and see how the devotion of Christians in past ages has been built into noble pillars and arches, carved into woodwork and sculpture. Think of the faith which inspired the building's design and the love which built it and the devotion which has preserved it; and see these outward things as signs and symbols of the continuing Divine Life which has been transforming men and women down the ages. Consider how the regular Eucharist, the daily psalms, the readings from scripture, the Sunday sermon have influenced and guided the thoughts and choices and habits of countless generations of ordinary people.

All this and much more has been handed on to us. It is for us to hand it on to our children, not just as we received it, unaltered, but added to by the self-sacrificing devotion of our own lives as we fulfil a Christian discipleship in our own times.

But if we take our past for granted, never reflect on it, nor try to understand what our special inheritance is, we shall never value it as we ought. It will neither influence us as it should nor will we hand it on enriched to future ages. Consider then in brief outline some of the ways in which we in our English Church have received and shaped and handed on the same single Catholic faith and worship and way of life brought to us by the Celtic saints from Ireland and by St Augustine of Canterbury from the continent of Europe.

The Church of England is the Church of the British people. As we British are a mixed people, so our Church tradition is also a mixed tradition. It has been our destiny in recent years to form contacts with other people in every corner of the globe – in places undreamt of by those who built our ancient churches. In India, Africa, the Far East today, the Anglican Church is face to face with all the religions and cultures of the world. The fact that this Church which went out from England now numbers among its members people of so many races and cultures is a strong contemporary proof that it is a true part of the Catholic Church – of the Church of Christ which is *universal* in character, drawing to him men and women of all nations. But just as these contacts today are enriching our Christian experience – so in the past we have continuously received from other parts of Christendom.

Rome sent us St Augustine and brought our island into touch with the rich heritage of the Western Church. The Irish and Scottish saints – Columba, Aidan, Cuthbert – brought us a pattern of simplicity in holiness which has been one of the threads of gold in our tapestry. From the Greek Church of the East came Archbishop Theodore of Tarsus, who gave us the parochial system and our Anglican ideal of a resident priest in every community. Thus was forged a link of friendship between our Church and the Orthodox Churches of the East which in many ways is closer now than it has ever been.

When the Reformation came upon us 400 years ago and, in a famous phrase, the English Church was made to look again in the mirror of Scripture and to wash its face, Protestant refugees from the Continent came to England. A hundred years later English churchmen spent many years as refugees abroad. These events led to a richer fusion of ideas and experiences and personalities in English Christianity than anywhere else. We learned a great deal from those Continental Christians. Others came about 200 years ago – Huguenot refugees from France; still more have come in recent years. But we have never believed everything that our visitors have tried to persuade us – be they Romans or Lutherans or Calvinists. We have taken something from them all and have woven it into our tapestry, but in a dogged insular fashion we have designed our own distinct pattern of life and worship.

We have never forgotten – as Protestants have tended to forget – that the one holy Catholic and Apostolic Church is built on the foundation of apostles and prophets, Jesus Christ being the chief cornerstone, and has a continuous history. We have never ceased to feel ourselves at one in essential faith and order with the great communions of East and West or to grieve when, like Rome until recently, they have refused to acknowledge our credentials.

Therefore our English Church is not called after any one man – as is the case with Lutherans and Calvinists; nor is our respect for the see of Canterbury in any way to be compared with the submission of others to the Bishop of Rome. No one man and no one party has been able to fix and stereotype our worship or our way of life; and we have not been afraid to allow sound reason and scholarship to lead us into fuller understanding of the Bible documents in which our faith is enshrined.

So by the grace of God acting through changing historical circumstance Anglicanism has emerged as a distinct version of Christianity in a divided Church.

We have a freedom to reach back behind the Reformation and draw upon the rich treasure-store of Catholic tradition; the Oxford Movement in the last century stimulated these rediscoveries of our heritage. We have a freedom to scrutinise our life in the light of the Bible – a freedom given to us by the Reformation and under the influence of the Wesleys and the Evangelical Revival, deepening to personal faith and devotion of individuals. We have a freedom to keep abreast of the new discoveries and problems of each new generation, believing that all truth in the end meets in God – a freedom given to us by the men of new learning at the Renaissance.

In recalling these influences that have made us what we are, we are recalling the past not out of boastfulness or complacency but in order that we may have our loyalty strengthened by understanding, our religious habits reinforced by conviction. Our sense of vocation and mission is deepened and extended as we come to know better what we are and what God would have us be.

To be an Anglican is not easy. To live and worship in a Church which contains within itself such a variety of Christian thought and experience calls for a mature faith. But ours is a splendid vocation. In other parts of Christendom the different denominations were distinct, with walls between them. You only leaped over if you wanted to change one religious allegiance for another. In our Anglican communion the best insights, traditions, practices of these separated Christians are mingled together in our common life and worship.

The Anglican Church itself is the greatest experiment so far in Christian unity. I believe this under God to be its distinctive vocation. We are what we are because we try to hold together in one communion, in love and unity, as wide a variety of Christian experience as is compatible with loyalty to the mainstream of historic Christianity. We are the standing proof that Catholics, Evangelicals and liberals can all live together as members of one organic body. We have become a meeting place in a divided Church.

We have under God become the one Church in Christendom where antiquity and modernity, East and West, Catholic and Evangelical can meet and converse and worship together. All this makes a great demand on patience, humility and charity. We have not yet as a Church risen to the height of these demands and opportunities. But insofar as we allow ourselves in the Church of England to understand each other, to speak the truth to one another in love, so we shall be able to help Orthodox and Protestant and Papist to meet each other and come to recognise in each other the true members of the Lord Jesus. We cannot just remain as we are; we must always be seeking for our own deeper unity as Anglicans; and we shall find that the more readily if we work for the wider unity into which at last all our separate existences as Churches will be merged when we all meet in the restored Eucharist of the undivided Church.

We should learn from a better understanding of our past, present and destined future to be Anglicans not just from accident of birth or habit of membership, but Anglicans by a sense of vocation and the conviction that has inspired countless consecrated lives in the past and will again in the future. The spirit of Anglican conviction is finely expressed in these words of Robert Sanderson, who was Bishop of Lincoln in the first years of the reign of Charles II and to whose pen we owe the Preface to the Book of Common Prayer.

> And here I do profess, that as I have lived, so I desire, and (by the Grace of God) resolve to die, in the Communion of the Catholic Church of Christ and a true son of the Church of England: which as it stands by law established to be both in doctrine and worship agreeable to the word of God, and in the most material points of both conformable to the faith and practice of the godly churches of Christ

in the primitive and purer times, I do firmly believe; led so to do, not so much from the force of custom and education (to which the greatest part of mankind owe their particular different persuasions in point of religion,) as upon the clear evidence of truth and reason. Wherefore I humbly beseech Almighty God the Father of mercies to preserve the Church by his power and providence in peace, truth, and godliness evermore unto the world's end.